HOW TO MAKE
CHILDREN'S FURNITURE AND PLAY EQUIPMENT

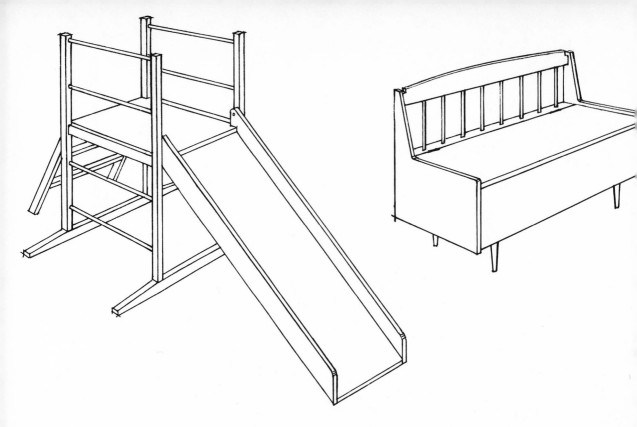

HOW TO MAKE

Mario Dal Fabbro

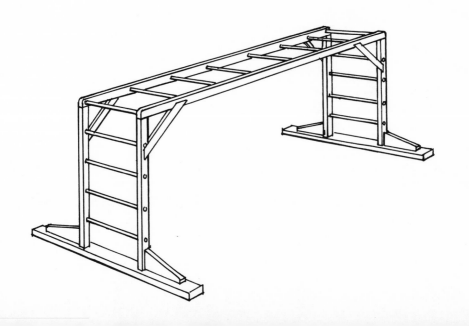

CHILDREN'S FURNITURE
AND PLAY EQUIPMENT

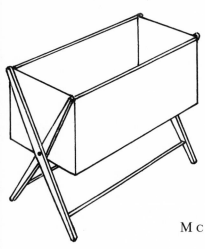

McGRAW-HILL BOOK COMPANY, INC.

New York   Toronto   London

PREFACE

This volume, the third in my "How to Build" series, is really a book for children and teen-agers, even though it can be used only by adults. To clarify this seeming paradox we must explain that its purpose is to help the home craftsman, amateur hobbyist and do-it-yourselfer to build the kind of furniture and play equipment that most children and teen-agers would like to have—both inside and outside the home.

All of the sixty projects covered in the book fill basic needs in the nursery, basement play room, bedroom, and backyard play area. Each has been designed and tested in accordance with the basic principles established in the preceding two books, *How to Build Modern Furniture* and *How to Make Built-in Furniture*, both of which have been very successful in the United States and abroad. These principles are simplicity of design, sturdiness of construction, low cost of materials, and ease of assembly. Text and drawings have been integrated to make each project completely self-explanatory. To make the reader's choice somewhat easier, all projects have been grouped into seven general classifications or sections—beds, tables, storage units, indoor equipment, outdoor equipment, etc.

Preceding the actual projects is a general introduction containing the highly informative essay, "The Child's World," by Jessie Stanton and Irma Simonton Black, which clearly establishes the psychological principles underlying the book as a whole, followed by a short review of general instructions—such as how to buy wood, how to read drawings, the type of hardware used, the more common wood joints employed, pointers on child safety, and the like.

The second part of the book, beginning on page 30, tells how to build sixty different projects, ranging from a simple plywood chair to a professional-type outdoor trampoline—from standard construction blocks to a full-size desk, a wardrobe and chifforobe, and a big outdoor playhouse that doubles as a roomy storage shed. Each project is presented clearly and simply, yet with as many drawings as deemed necessary for full and complete visualization and assembly—scale drawings, perspective drawings, exploded isometric drawings, enlarged detail drawings, lists of materials with dimensions, and numbered instructions for assembling.

Besides the obvious saving in cost over store-bought furniture and equipment, the home craftsman and hobbyist—be it Dad or Mom, Aunt Jo or Uncle Henry—will derive much more than the usual satisfaction at having created these pieces himself. He will have as an additional reward the happy smiles of the children and teen-agers who will enjoy them, and the knowledge that his handiwork has brightened and enlarged their lives—educationally as well as recreationally.

The projects will indeed provide fun for both maker and user. In this way the book should, it is hoped, make some contribution to better living in the child's world.

New York
October, 1962   MARIO DAL FABBRO

CONTENTS

SECTION 7: OUTDOOR PLAY EQUIPMENT

HOW TO MAKE
CHILDREN'S FURNITURE AND PLAY EQUIPMENT

THE CHILD'S WORLD

By Jessie Stanton and Irma Simonton Black
The Bank Street School of Education,
New York City

Imagine yourself in a world where a giant had to lift you on to a chair, and where your legs always dangled in the air when you sat. Imagine a world in which you had to stand on tiptoe to see what was being served for dinner, and where your first glimpse of visiting friends was their legs.

This is the world in which young children live all the time. Obviously it is impossible to scale the rest of the world to fit them, to make all houses exclusively for children. Yet we can provide many spots where chairs, tables and child match in size. Low chairs and a low table where a child and his friend may sit with feet resting comfortably on the floor are a must, as well as low shelves where they may see toys attractively arranged and reach them easily.

For that matter, attractively designed, sturdy furniture and equipment is a satisfaction at any age. Even to a very young child such material is esthetically pleasing. The simplicity and excellent proportion of the designs given in this book will not only please a child but will also be a factor in shaping his own tastes.

It is the book's purpose to provide detailed suggestions and plans for creating a comfortable, usable and pleasant place in which a child may live and play. One of the advantages of much of the equipment pictured here is that it may be used in a variety of ways as the child's needs change. The open shelves that once held blocks become a place for books and model airplanes. The toy chest that was the home of stuffed animals becomes a storage place for boxed games or equipment such as bats, baseball gloves, and the like. The outdoor playhouse makes an excellent toolshed.

The same cannot be said, of course, of some of the furniture designs—cribs, play pens, low chairs and the like (Sections 1 and 2). But if these things do not serve the same child at different interest levels, they can serve different children at the same age. And it's a great day for Junior, who may have some regrets about letting the new baby inherit his cozy crib, when he moves into a youth bed that Daddy built especially for him (Project 2.4), complete with attractive headboard that will hold books and toys.

The kind of place a child's room can be—the amount and arrangement of his furniture and indoor and outdoor play equipment—will naturally vary with family tastes and budget. Yet to a surprising extent children have very similar needs because they have similar characteristics. If the fathers and mothers who spend creative energy and time on making a child's room comfortable and attractive are aware of some of these general characteristics of childhood, they will be able to provide opportunities for active play and learning in pleasing surroundings at each stage of a child's life. This introduction provides a picture of children at various stages of development, with particular reference to the kinds of play opportunities and play materials most suited to the growing child.

Sensory Experience and Physical Activity

It is almost impossible for adults to realize how much young children have to learn. The adult recognizes perspective and knows that the tree that looks so little to him is several blocks away. Familiar with the feel and texture of many objects, he dismisses them casually as he touches them. But the young child can stroke a piece of soft velvet in the full delight of a sensory pleasure discovered for the first time.

Much of the seemingly undirected activity of the early years of childhood is really a learning experience. A three-year-old rode his kiddie kar up against a closed door, stood up—still straddling his kiddie kar—and tried to pull the door open. After several ineffectual attempts to open the door, he realized that he himself was in the way. He got off the kiddie kar, moved it out of the way and pulled the door open with ease. Of course, he could not have formulated this problem-solution into a theory about opposing objects—much less put it into words. But all the same he showed by his action that he had learned a basic principle.

It is largely through action, through trial and error, that children learn the way things work. Provision for such activity is, therefore, provision for learning.

As a child grows older his learnings become more complex. Each successive experience is no longer a discovery; he begins to abstract from many experiences certain general principles. He may discover for himself that a seesaw with equal weights on the ends will remain horizontal. He may discover with some surprise that the snow he put in his pocket turns to water. Through such repeated experiences with physical phenomena the young child discovers a number of elementary physical laws. The child who has had experiences of this kind in his preschool years will most likely be eager to learn in school. Now he learns through books while continuing to learn through direct experience and physical activity.

The Child's World

Slides (6.9, 7.11) and ladders (6.10, 7.8, 7.9) give children the chance to experiment, to venture. The child who rides high in a swing (7.7, 7.8) will look down at his world with a new perspective, figuratively and literally.

Throughout the preschool years and after, a child needs the chance to use his entire body—running, climbing, jumping and in other big-muscle activities. The school-age child will do these things for the pure joy of using his body and will invent endless variations on such simple basic activities as climbing, swinging or sliding.

The preschool and the elementary school child's need for physical activity should be considered in arranging his room and in selecting his play materials. For one thing, he needs space. This does not mean that he has to live on a prairie in order to grow up strong and alert, but simply that he should have as much uncluttered floor space as possible for active play.

Many of the pieces of equipment suggested in this book are designed so as to facilitate play by getting toys and play equipment off the floor and on to appropriate places around walls. Modular bookshelves or storage pieces (3.2) provide an attractive place for display as well as storage for toys. The handsome Junior bed and headboard (2.4) will offer encouragement to even the most haphazard youngster to keep his possessions organized. The decorative toyshelf-storage cabinet (5.4), the neat bookshelves (5.6), the display cabinet (5.7)—all offer inviting spots for keeping equipment belonging to a child at once available and orderly. (For a fuller discussion of room arrangement, see p. 9.)

Self-Expression Through Play

Good indoor play equipment leads to many kinds of expressive and dramatic play. Provision for such play with art or plastic materials is relatively simple to make.

A set of construction blocks (6.2) with small cars, trains, animals and people is basic, and will be used by children from two years right on through the middle years. Eight- and nine-year-olds may enjoy building elaborate and artistic block structures at home. The blocks should be stored on open shelves (3.2, 5.4).

Bright poster paints in jars, along with brushes of varying sizes—long, wide ones for the younger children, smaller ones for more delicate work for older children—are best used at an easel (6.4). This provides the most satisfactory stance for painting with a free sweep of arm and shoulder. Painting on floor or table may encourage a cramped technique, more suitable for writing than for artwork.

Crayons, colored chalks, colored pencils, finger paints are all interesting media for work with color and form.

Regular modeling clay and plasticene, which is clay with an oil base, are excellent table materials. Both may be bought by the pound. If they are used on a breadboard or a piece of oilcloth, there will be practically no mess to clean up. A low table (4.5) and chair (4.9) offer the best location for such activities.

A workbench (4.13) provides for many kinds of learning. While a separate workbench is not absolutely necessary, it will go far toward helping a do-it-yourself parent to keep his sanity and to prevent an overeager youngster from premature use of complex or delicate tools. And surely any father who has made a beautiful piece of furniture will agree that woodworking is an art form! Incidentally, girls as well as boys enjoy learning skills of this kind.

Dramatic Play

One of the most important forms of play is usually referred to by educators as "dramatic play." This activity is absolutely universal among children, from the little girl who tenderly mothers her dolls to the shouting gang of nine-year-old boys who are playing cowboys and Indians. A young child whose imagination has been caught by airplanes, for instance, will *become* an airplane, zooming around the room and slowing to land. He may engage in other kinds of dramatic play about airplanes as well. He may make a horizontal ladder (7.9) into a plane, with himself as pilot and his friends as navigator and passengers. He may build a small airplane out of wood and construct an airport out of blocks. Any theme may be carried out in dramatic play at various levels of complexity. This play becomes extraordinarily real to a child. He is pretending, of course, but is hardly aware of it because he is so intensely absorbed. One five-year-old, who had made a small boat at the workbench, was pushing it across the floor of the schoolroom. Suddenly he looked up at his teacher with a delightful smile. "Can you hear the water lapping?" he asked softly.

In another instance a little boy and girl had been building a block farm and playing with it for several days. One morning the little boy arrived early, went to the barn and started to "milk" the cows. When his little friend arrived, he called her to come and help him. "I will not," she said, "I'm sick of the smell of those animals."

The folding playhouse (6.5) is excellent as a base for housekeeping play, and may be particularly useful on rainy days or during the short days of winter. It is also useful outdoors in the summer. Such a playhouse need not be restricted to domestic play. Boys will use it for a garage, as an Army headquarters, or in any number of offbeat ways.

A real outdoor playhouse (7.1) will especially delight a little girl in the years from about five to ten. As with the folding playhouse, this one need not be restricted to housekeeping play. Younger children should not be allowed to remain in any spot that shuts them off from occasional adult supervision. But even before a playhouse is used for dramatic play, it is excellent for storage of tricycles and other outdoor toys which must be protected from the weather. After its use as a playhouse is past, it will again offer shelter for bicycles, skates and all the other equipment that frequently clutters up garages or utility rooms.

A play interest shared by practically all children is the collection of an odd assortment of "treasures" that may seem utterly worthless to unimaginative adults. A young child's treasures may include a shiny button, a marble with a spiral twist inside of it, a piece of satin or velvet, pictures, shells and any other imaginable oddment you can think of. The young child's devotion to these things is real and should be respected.

Actually this collecting mania can mature into some very important interests in the later elementary and high school years. The stamp collection of the ten-year-old, or the model train and automobile collection that a twelve-year-old puts together with painstaking devotion, the miniature animals collected by an eleven-year-old girl are worthy interests, deserving of adult encouragement. The mature scientist who collects and identifies insects, ores or molds, and makes a contribution to medicine or to the physical sciences through his efforts, is motivated in part by much the same impulse to observe, to collect, to compare. Many of the furniture items pictured in this book are excellent for housing collections, and by their very nature help the child collector to organize his possessions. The bookshelves (5.6) and display cabinet (5.7), as well as other cabinets and shelves, are all flexible enough to be put to several different uses. As has been mentioned, uses may change as a child matures. All of the storage units in this book will serve from early childhood right on through the adolescent years.

One characteristic of practically all play is repetition. Young children repeat physical patterns endlessly. They climb up a slide and zoom down with as much glee on the twentieth time as the first. They practice skipping or skating over and over again. They put the same puzzle together over and over again.

If we look at this repetition of activities as learning experience, it becomes more understandable to us as adults. Anyone who has practiced "now is the time for all good men to come to the aid of the party" on a typewriter will know that it takes hundreds of repetitions before the sentence comes out quickly and smoothly. Or take any musical instrument: how can anyone acquire competence on piano or guitar without steady repetitive—indeed monotonous —practice? So the young child repeats physical and mental activities alike until they become second nature to him.

Not all repetition is mechanical, however. Children use the same play materials over and over, day after day (which is all the more reason for giving them sturdy, well-designed ones). They pounce on the blocks with eagerness, but they may build a skyscraper one day, a four-lane highway the next, and an animal hospital at still another time. The child who runs to the easel the first thing each morning is likely to do a fine abstract design one day and a space rocket the next. Or a group of children may play "store" with an accumulation of treasures, but they may play it with increasing realism and accuracy.

Outdoor Play

With a few exceptions the discussion so far has centered around indoor play. A child's room is the very core of his activity in a very personal and pleasant way. Yet of course every child needs to supplement his indoor play by outdoor activities in park, yard or playground. The family who can have a yard as an adjunct to the indoor play space is indeed fortunate. And the way the yard is equipped will determine to a great extent how much and with what satisfaction a child will use it.

A yard with enough space so that a child can run and jump, and with play equipment that can be pulled, pushed or climbed on will satisfy the child's need for strenuous activity. The very fact that outdoor activity is strenuous and the equipment is made largely to encourage the use of the large muscles means that outdoor play usually requires more supervision than indoor play.

A slide (7.11) is an excellent piece of equipment for climbing and then the fun of zooming down. Though sliding may seem to be merely fun, it actually requires a good deal of physical coordination. Children from about the age of four go down frontwards, backwards, sitting, or lying down. They may start slow and speed up, or start fast and brake with their feet along the edges of the slide.

The trampoline (7.6) is fine for many activities. Small children will use it for jumping or bouncing; school-age children who practice may master all sorts of somersaults. Parallel bars (7.4), consisting of two bars on a firm base, are good equipment for the development of a number of physical skills, ranging from "skinning the cat" to chinning oneself.

The three-way ladder (7.9) offers exciting opportunity for climbing, and is a fine piece of equipment for dramatic play. Combined with large hollow blocks and light, smooth, planks, an ingenious structure like this may become anything from a house or a bridge to a space satellite.

In addition to these play materials which parents can build themselves, they may want to add such manufactured "regulars" as tricycles, carts, large inflated balls and the like.

Children also enjoy the relaxing pleasure of rhythmic motion. Swings, rings, and rocking devices of various kinds are enjoyed by children from infancy well into the school years. These are by no means passive pleasures. A simple swing may be enjoyed lazily, it is true, but it may also provide vigorous sport when two children stand on it and "pump" in opposite directions.

A seesaw (7.8) is good for children of five or older, but may be dangerous for preschool children unless carefully supervised. If one child gets off suddenly, the other one may be badly jolted. The rocking boat (7.12) may be used for the sheer physical fun of rocking, or turned into an energetic dramatic play of a storm at sea. When preschoolers are using this item, parents should keep other small children at a safe distance.

Much of this outdoor equipment may be used indoors during prolonged spells or bad weather. If there is a basement or game room available all but the largest pieces or those that are anchored to the ground, may be taken indoors. Especially good for babies is the small slide (6.9).

Room Arrangement

After the chore of building sturdy furniture and play equipment is over and your child's room looks like something out of *House and Garden,* you may think you can relax. Actually you are just beginning. Arranging furniture and equipment to the best advantage, and keeping it arranged, are just as important as building it. The child's need for floor space has been mentioned previously. Even in a small room this may be materially increased by putting tables, chairs and other furniture against the wall rather than in the middle of the room. In a very small room it may be possible to increase floor space by building a table that is hinged to the wall. Cabinets with doors containing play material that requires adult assistance may be placed above the open shelves that are always in a child's reach. Bulletin and chalk boards (3.4) and special cabinets (5.9) provide space for a child's paintings, clippings, and chalk work without cluttering precious shelf or table space. Walls can be liberally lined with shelves and other storage units (3.2, 5.6) chosen from the various designs in this book, according to individual family tastes.

The floor space can be more effectively used if it is not broken up by coverings such as small rugs. A smooth clear surface is essential for almost any active play. Balancing blocks or using push-toys on a crumply rug is extremely frustrating. Inlaid linoleum or tiles of various composition are good for the child's play and are also easy to keep clean. A party with two or three children and real lemonade and cookies may create much hilarity and also some spills. The spills need not be serious if the floor covering is waterproof. The same thing goes for water color paints, finger paints and other messy materials which are nevertheless invaluable in providing change and relaxation.

From Six to Ten

As a child grows into the middle years—from six to ten—he usually remains energetic and physically active, but his activity takes more focused and directed forms. These are the years for organized games (see the folding Ping-pong table, 6.7), for the beginning of collecting, for more complex dramatic play.

Now he begins to need less floor space and more work space such as desks, tables, tools, and benches. For a time he will combine his grown-up equipment and interest with the equipment and interests of earlier years. Books will be side-by-side with blocks and toy animals and dolls. But for a long time he will need space for energetic play with toy trucks and complicated electric train setups.

If space permits, a permanent train platform is fine, and provides a chance for boys through the high school years to engage in elaborate train play, complete with switches, lights, bridges, and stations.

And as we have seen, girls in the middle years need space for complex dramatic play with dolls, miniature furniture and other housekeeping equipment.

A plywood strip installed around the playroom wall (p. 22) is excellent as a place on which to tack paintings, cutouts, crayon drawings and all sorts of juvenile productions. Keep the collection moving and it will be more interesting. As a matter of fact, a child's own paintings make surprisingly attractive wall decorations if the rest of the décor is kept simple. And it also gives a child a feeling of pride in his work.

Later on the plywood strip may be used as a sort of bulletin board for an older child. Clips from newspapers, special pictures of interest from magazines—even lists of chores—may be thumbtacked up temporarily.

A real bulletin board (3.4) is useful for special projects.

The toy chest, which is here designed to double as bench as well (5.5), requires a word of warning. If it is used for large, soft objects such as stuffed animals, dolls and the like, it has a legitimate place. But if it is used as a repository for ill-assorted collection of large, small and discarded toys, deposited helter-skelter, it is a snare and a delusion. It is always a temptation to a busy adult to open a lid or a door, and deposit in a heap the inevitable litter that results from active play. It is a temptation one should resist.

The young child needs to have his toys and play equipment organized. Materials that he uses every day—blocks, trains, trucks, and other transportation toys, toy animals and people, dolls, doll dishes, wooden puzzles, etc.— should be grouped together on low shelves. The sight of a toy trailer-truck may inspire a little boy to set up a complicated highway of blocks, complete with bridges and toll gates. The sight of a family of toy people may give a little girl the idea of starting a complex housekeeping play, with the father going out to work, the mother taking care of the children or going shopping to the grocery store.

While low shelves are a must for materials that the child can handle by himself and is likely to use practically every day, high shelves (perhaps with doors) are also useful in the early years even where space is ample. Preschool children cannot manage paste and scissors or paints without some adult supervision. They scatter the parts of puzzles under radiators or lose them in the depths of doll carriages. The radiator cover (3.1) will be useful in this connection as well as for safety. The sensible precaution of placing such things well out of a child's reach insures both his safety and future happiness—since he is usually just as upset as his parents if he breaks or loses something precious. Other material that may be kept out of reach are toys that the child seldom uses or toys that may be the fresher and more appealing if out of sight for a few days or weeks.

Excess toys resulting from a huge haul at birthday or Christmas may also be profitably put away for a spell. Children who are overrich in quantity of toys are just as likely as adults who are overrich in money to be bored with excess and to flit from one activity to another. Moreover, since many gifts from well-meaning friends are beyond the child's ability to use, they are likely to induce frustration as well as boredom. The interlocking jigsaw puzzle designed for grownups may be held until the child is older, or saved for a rainy day when he may use it with the assistance of an adult or older child. By the time a child is able to manage all of his possessions single-handedly, he will be glad to have both low and high shelves for the play equipment, collections of various kinds, books, records and all the other paraphernalia he will probably have acquired.

It is quite legitimate to expect a child, even as young as three, to help in some way with straightening up. Hand him little piles of blocks to put back on the shelves. Suggest that he put crayons back in the box. Be ready to appreciate any efforts he makes on his own, but don't act as if he were doing you a favor. A child who from the beginning is helped to establish order in his own domain is apt to keep on liking a pleasantly tidy place to work even when he takes entire charge of the operation.

When a child is five or under the quality of his play will be much better if he is helped to clear up his room twice daily—before the midday meal and before supper. This may seem like an unnecessary chore to a busy mother, and of course she may have to skip it part of the time. But when such clean-up work is possible, a child will emerge from rest and get back to play—"work"— with greater zest if he can step into a cleared room and select a new arrangement of playthings. Any adult who has left a party clutter of ash trays, dishes and glasses until the next morning will know the dim view that a child may take of a room that is littered with the remnants of the morning's activity.

It may come as something of a disappointment to a father who has struggled to create a pleasant and usable room for his children—and to the mother who has abetted if not aided him—that the child does not at once use it as the center of most of his activities. The fact is that the little child literally does not have enough differentiated "self" to work and play alone. Occasionally the two- or three-year-old may become totally absorbed in some activity on his own. Perhaps it is a new set of paints, a new doll, a new pound of clay that keeps him glued to chair or floor for five to twenty minutes. Playing with other children may accomplish the same miracle. But usually he wants mother or a mother-substitute close at hand. He keeps coming back to her like Antaeus came to his mother, earth, to obtain strength, ideas, and peace of mind.

A Dutch door (page 22) may permit a child to begin to enjoy the pleasure of playing by himself in his room and yet talk back and forth to his mother. It should not, however, be used as a way to keep him penned in against his will. The Dutch door is also useful for the child with a baby brother or sister who appropriates his belongings.

At five or six the child may play by himself for relatively long periods, and with a friend he may remain absorbed for an entire morning or afternoon, although it is probable that even now some adult will be needed to unsnarl tangled ideas and wills from time to time.

Still later, from the later elementary years on to adulthood, every child is entitled to some period of absolute privacy—a time when he may retire to his room for reading or play or simply for daydreaming. Long school hours, lessons of many kinds after school, some responsibility for helping around the house, organized activities such as Scouts, teams of various kinds—all these leave small time for being alone, for thinking and dreaming. When a child arrives at the stage where he seeks privacy, even if only occasionally, the wise parent will see that he has a time and place in which to enjoy it.

And, of course, one of the most important factors to consider in setting up a child's room, and in building his equipment, is safety. As in every other topic related to children, safety is related to the child's stage of development. The infant or toddler must have pretty constant supervision. Every parent expects to watch out for the very young child because he knows that the child has absolutely no judgment. But when a child gets to be three or four or five, many parents think that he is now competent to take care of himself. In many ways he is. But he still needs safeguards for a surprisingly long time. Children concentrate so deeply on what they are doing that they may be completely unaware of potential dangers.

Some simple principles of safety include having shelves securely fastened to the wall, or else wide enough so that they will not topple over. A youngster who is eager to reach a toy won't think of the dangers involved in climbing up an unstable set of shelves.

A simple step stool of one or two steps gives a child added reaching ability and also insures his safety (4.10). And the very young child will enjoy climbing the steps just for the fun of climbing.

In building or selecting furniture or play equipment, avoid sharp points or corners. And be sure to select a paint that is nontoxic and nonpoisonous. The chief offender is the usual exterior paint which contains lead in amounts dangerous to health if a child chews or sucks it. This precaution is wise for children through the preschool years. It is amazing how many children will mouth a toy when they are long past the baby stage.

Outdoor equipment usually needs supervision longer than does indoor equipment. A youngster eager to slide may unthinkingly push another one perched on the top. A child enjoying a high, vigorous swing is a hazard to one who may run past at the wrong moment.

So far as possible the equipment mentioned in this book has been designed with safety in mind. Yet it is never possible to provide complete safety without some judicious adult supervision.

Safety is important, just as is a seatbelt in a plane. But it has nothing to do with the actual flight. In addition to safety, the equipment suggested here is intended to give to a child the motive to use his own wings—of imagination, of reason, of delight in his own unique and growing abilities.

SELECTING AND BUYING WOOD

After the design has been selected and studied, the next step is the ordering of material. One method is to buy the lumber in standard lengths and cut the required pieces as listed. Another method is to ask the lumber dealer to cut the material into the sizes you need. There will be a minimum of waste whichever method is used, because standard lumber sizes have been considered in the planning of the designs.

Except for edge treatment, avoid using solid wood and plywood together in the same piece of furniture, particularly if a flush board is to be visible. If such a combination of materials is unavoidable, glue should never be used for bonding the parts. Plywood and solid wood react differently to drying glue and to atmospheric conditions, but screws or loose joints will permit shrinkage or expansion. Another point to keep in mind is that both soft and hard wood shrink in the process of seasoning. Thus the wood is usually ⅟₁₆ in. narrower than the nominal thickness. This difference is of consequence only in fitting such parts as doors, shelves or drawers. If the wood is of a different thickness from that specified in the design, adjustments must be made in the dimensions of the part to be applied. Therefore it is best to secure lumber of a thickness as close as possible to that specified.

CUTTING AND ASSEMBLING THE PARTS

Whether wood is shaped by hand or by use of woodworking machines, the process consists of removing small parts of wood by sawing, planing, or chiseling in accordance with the selected design.

After the design has been studied and suitable wood selected, the various pieces can be traced directly on the wood for cutting. The parts should be laid out in such a way that the handsomest surfaces of the wood will be seen in the finished piece. In the cutting operation itself, accuracy is very important; if the parts are to fit together as designed, the lumber must be cut at the correct angle. The saw cut should fall *outside* the pencil line, so that the board can be planed or filed to correct dimensions. (A plane is used on flat surfaces, and a file on curved edges.)

When the parts have been cut and finished to the right sizes, the joints may be marked and executed as indicated in the details. Sometimes it is possible to save time by eliminating the joint and substituting nails. Before any parts are joined, all should be checked to make sure they will fit.

Instructions for assembly are provided with each design. The glue must be spread on both surfaces to be joined, and the pieces clamped together for several hours. Simple clamps or screws and nails may be used to apply pressure. Wood clamps may be made by nailing blocks of wood to the ends of a rail slightly longer than the piece being glued, and applying pressure by inserting wedges between the wood and the blocks.

Large assemblies

Before assembling a large piece of furniture, particularly a built-in unit, it is wise to measure passageways to make sure it can be moved from the shop to the site that has been picked for it. It may be necessary to assemble the piece in two or three units in the shop, and complete the assembly in the room where the piece is to be installed.

WOOD FINISH

The kind of finish a piece of furniture should receive will depend upon the quality and appearance of the wood, the use it will receive, decorating tastes, and so on. Nothing shows off the beauty of the wood—and the builder's achievement!—quite so well as a "natural" finish. Or it may seem preferable to add a touch of bright color to the decorating scheme of a room by painting the piece. Nowadays furniture makers sometimes achieve bold, striking effects by the carefully planned use of contrasting panels on the same piece: for example, the drawer fronts of a chest might be enameled or lacquered pure white, while the frame could be a strong, deep tone of almost any other color that would "go well" in the room. A word of caution to the amateur decorator: if you lack confidence in your judgment, or are wavering between color and natural finish, remember that the latter is never in bad taste. Furthermore, a natural finish can later be painted over if you find you are not happy with it. It is a far more difficult proposition to remove paint if you later decide you prefer the "natural" look.

The subject of wood finishing is too extensive to receive adequate treatment here, but a few general pointers are worth giving:

Carefully sand smooth all surfaces, both before and between coats of finish. Grade 2/0 sandpaper is recommended for raw wood; finer grades of waterproof sandpaper —such as 4/0 or 6/0—are suitable between finish coats, and may be dipped in water to prevent clogging and minimize dust. Other methods of smoothing the surfaces, such as rubbing with fine steel wool, pumice, or other fine abrasives, may also be used. Dust should be allowed to settle before liquid finishes are applied, and the air in the workroom should be clear and still. Be sure that a coat of finish is thoroughly dry before sanding and proceeding with the next coat, and never rub or sand the final coat of paint or enamel. Various rubbing compounds or 8/0 sandpaper may be sparingly used after the final coat of shellac or varnish.

Preparation of surface

Most raw woods need careful preparation before they can be painted or finished. Neglect of this essential preliminary will not only increase the number of coats necessary to obtain proper coverage—with consequent waste of materials and labor— but will produce less satisfactory results. Fillers, primers, and undercoats are not cheaper types of finishing material to be used where they won't "show"—they are indispensable components of a proper finish.

In applying finishes, use good brushes and keep them in good condition. It is best to keep special brushes for special uses: one brush for shellac, another for varnish, a third for lacquer. A nylon brush should not be used with shellac, as the alcohol solvent will attack the bristles.

Open-grained hardwoods—such as oak, birch, walnut, mahogany, cherry, elm, hickory, chestnut, or butternut—must be filled. If the wood is to be stained, this operation should precede filling or be combined with it—filler-stain preparations are available in a number of shades. If wood filler is applied separately, it should be brushed or wiped on and the excess rubbed off with a clean rag. It is important to follow the manufacturer's instructions faithfully with all finishing materials.

Close-grained woods—such as maple, pine, fir, gum, cedar, poplar, beech, basswood, or cottonwood—do not need to be filled, but a coat of thin shellac is recommended to seal fir before varnishing, because of the soft grain. If there are any knots or resin pockets in the wood, they should be sealed with shellac or knot-sealer.

Plastic wood or crack filler (in shades to match the wood, if a natural finish is selected) should be used to fill nail holes or crevices after they have been primed, either by the first finish coat or by swabbing with linseed oil or varnish.

Natural finishes

Among natural finishes, the least discoloration of the raw wood is obtained with wax, but this method also offers least protection against hard usage. A single coat of white shellac or clear varnish should precede the wax. Combined varnish-wax preparations are also available.

Clear lacquer can yield striking results, and there are now preparations available which make it possible to apply this traditionally difficult material with a brush instead of a spray-gun.

A "white" shellac finish will discolor wood less than varnish, but is not waterproof. A "5-lb cut" shellac contains five pounds of shellac gum to the gallon of alcohol; "4-lb cut" contains only four pounds. Either of these concentrations will give good results, but the "3-lb cut" frequently found in stores is not recommended, except for preliminary coats, which should be thin.

Varnish finish combines durability with the attractiveness of a natural finish. Spar varnish is suitable for pieces like kitchen cabinets that are exposed to moisture. Other types of varnish are suitable for high-gloss effects, and some types have pigment added to combine the coloring effect of paint with the natural grain of the wood.

Paint or enamel finish

If the wood is to be painted, it must first be primed, although some special formulations and most rubber-base paints are self-priming. If it is to be enameled, best results will be obtained by using an enamel undercoat preparation. It is generally advisable to mix a little of the finish coat into the white primer or enamel undercoat, in order to tint it, and provide a better base for the final pigment. This measure is especially advisable if the final color is very deep.

FITTING FURNITURE TO THE WALL

Usually 1 in. of space should be allowed between built-in furniture and the walls or ceiling. This space is filled with strips of wood, ½ to 1 in. wide on both sides of the piece and 1 in. around the top.

Boards that extend from wall to wall or from floor to ceiling must be measured exactly, following any irregularities.

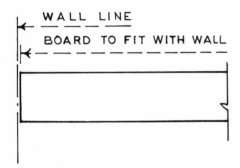

BOARD WALL TO WALL

WALL LINE
BOARD TO FIT WITH WALL

VARIABLE DIMENSIONS

Some of the furniture shown in this book has been planned to fit into a wide variety of room layouts and spaces. Naturally some of the dimensions will be determined by the space the pieces will occupy in the actual home. The calculation of such dimensions is given as follows:

Boards: Board that runs wall to wall must be cut to the precise dimensions of the room. Where a piece (or pieces) of known dimensions fills part of such span, the subtraction of the known dimensions from the length of wall-to-wall distance will be the length of the board or boards.

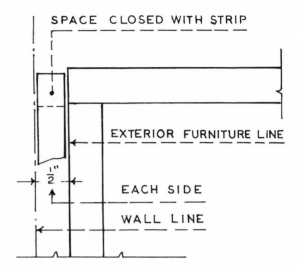

FRONT VIEW– FURNITURE WALL TO WALL

SPACE CLOSED WITH STRIP

EXTERIOR FURNITURE LINE

EACH SIDE

WALL LINE

$\frac{1}{2}$"

Furniture parts: Variable dimensions of cabinets, bookcases, etc. that run wall to wall can be determined by taking the dimension of the room wall to wall, as shown on this page. Follow the list of materials to calculate the dimension of every single part comprising the unit.

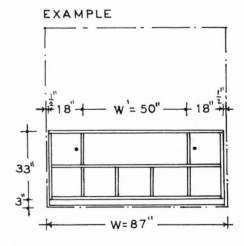

W = WIDTH OF THE ROOM
W' = WIDTH OF THE ROOM LESS 37"

EXAMPLE

18"   W' = 50"   18"

33"

3"

W = 87"

HARDWARE

The hardware illustrated in this book is standard and can be purchased in most hardware stores. Items frequently used are shown here to facilitate identification.

Springs and upholstery materials can be purchased in upholstery repair shops.

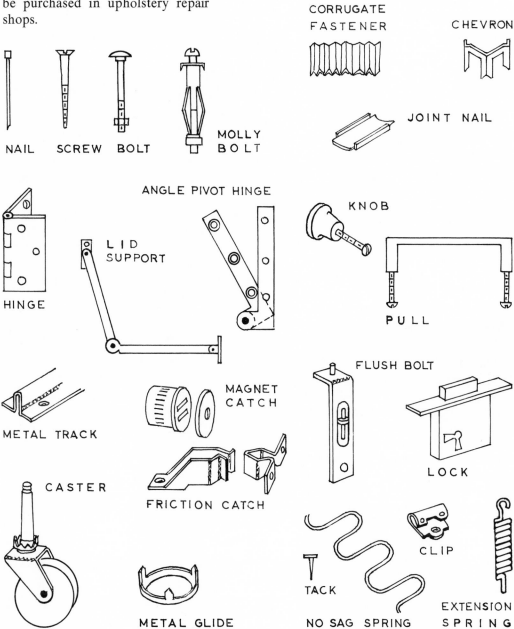

CORRUGATE FASTENER

CHEVRON

JOINT NAIL

NAIL   SCREW   BOLT

MOLLY BOLT

ANGLE PIVOT HINGE

LID SUPPORT

KNOB

HINGE

PULL

METAL TRACK

MAGNET CATCH

FLUSH BOLT

LOCK

CASTER

FRICTION CATCH

TACK

CLIP

NO SAG SPRING

EXTENSION SPRING

METAL GLIDE

MEDIUM WORKING HEIGHTS FOR CHILDREN AND TEEN-AGERS

A child's world, we have noted, is much different dimensionally from ours. While most of the projects in this book have been designed with this important fact in mind, the following table shows how working heights change as the child grows into adulthood. It should prove useful for do-it-yourself designers.

ITEM	MEDIUM WORKING HEIGHT, INCHES, BY AGE			
	4 to 7	7 to 11	11 to 14	14 to 18
CABINET, DISPLAY (TOP)	50	57	68	76
CHAIR AND BENCH	10	12	15	18
CHALKBOARD (BOTTOM)	22	25	31	36
DESK AND TABLE	18	21	26	29
DESK, TYPING			26	26
DOORKNOB	25	28	32	36
HOOK, COAT	35	45	56	66
LAVABO AND SINK	24	27	32	36
LIGHT SWITCH	27	35	50	65
MIRROR (BOTTOM)	35	39	46	52
PENCIL SHARPENER	27	32	40	48
SHELF, BOOKS	38	44	56	66
STOOL, DRAWING		21	24	26
TABLE, DRAWING		28	32	36
TABLE, WORK (STANDING)	26	28	32	36
TACKBOARD (BOTTOM)	22	25	31	36
TOWEL, SUPPORT	27	33	42	54
WINDOW EDGE	29	33	36	40

PROTECTION FOR CHILDREN

Most children don't know what danger is—any more than they know right from wrong. But all parents want to provide the maximum protection for their children when buying or building furniture and play equipment. Here are a few ideas that can be very useful in this regard.

ROUND ALL CORNERS

Square corners are a source of danger for children, especially on tables, where they are generally at eye level. "Soften up" all exposed corners by rounding them, either with coping saw or by cutting off a small triangle and rounding each new edge with sandpaper.

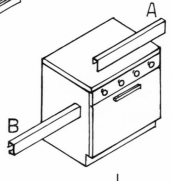

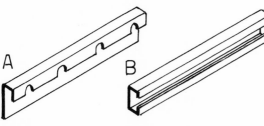

(SAFE) HOME ON THE RANGE

What child wouldn't play with the knobs on the gas range or electric oven in emulation of Mommy? Here's one way to discourage this hazardous pastime. Either of the two pieces A or B of bent sheetmetal can be adapted to fit most ranges.

FOLDING GATE FOR STAIR SAFETY

Widely used until such time as the youngster learns to open it for himself, this "pantograph" type folding gate keeps toddlers from falling downstairs.

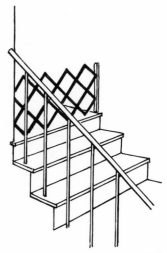

FOLDING GATE AS ROOM DIVIDER

The same folding gate shown on the preceding page can serve to keep the youngsters from roaming the house at will when Mother is preoccupied elsewhere. But it should never serve as prison bars for lonely tots.

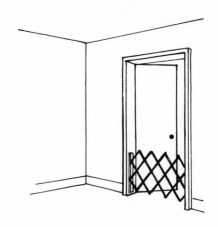

DUTCH DOOR

This serves the same principle as the folding gate, but is somewhat more elegant and definitely more permanent. Caution: make sure baby isn't behind the lower portion before you push it open!

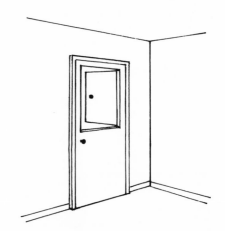

WALL PROTECTION

Children are natural-born muralists; armed with a soft wax crayon they can cover more wall area than a paperhanger. Protect their play room with varnished or painted plywood as indicated; you can also use it as a display and bulletin board.

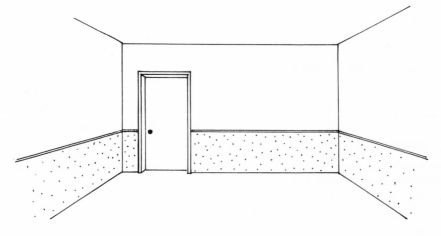

STANDARD DETAILS FOR DOOR INSTALLATION

Because the size of a door for any given opening will vary with the type of door used, the dimensions given in the lists of materials should be carefully checked to make sure that any necessary allowances are added for rabbetting, sliding door overlaps, or the like.

Doors with Butt Hinges

Standard doors are the most practical for use on furniture. These are easily hung on butt hinges by using a chisel and screwdriver.

The recessed door is most popular, because the recess hides any irregularity. Rabbet doors help to keep dust out of a cabinet. Offset hinges should be used to install heavy rabbet doors.

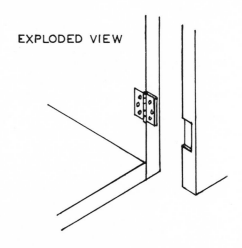

EXPLODED VIEW

PLAN SECTIONS

FLUSH DOORS

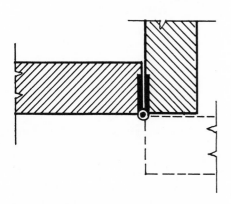

RECESSED DOORS

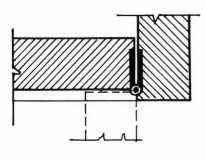

EXTERNAL DOORS

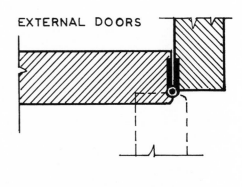

RABBET DOORS

ADD $\frac{3}{8}''$ ALL AROUND FOR RABBET

OFFSET HINGE

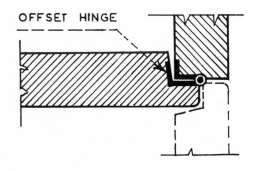

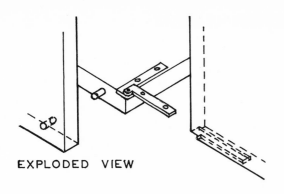

EXPLODED VIEW

PIVOT DOORS

Standard doors for cabinets may be hung with pivot hinges, which are concealed at top and bottom of door and allow it to pivot a full 180 degrees. The accompanying sketches show both normal and corner-pivot installations, neither of which presents any difficulty.

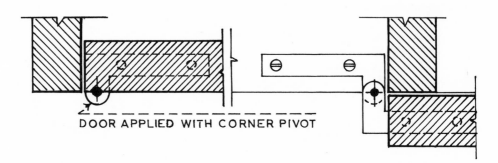

DOOR APPLIED WITH CORNER PIVOT

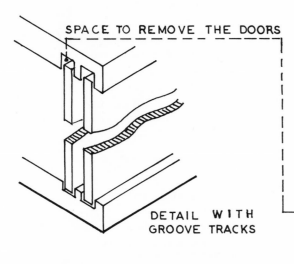

SPACE TO REMOVE THE DOORS

DETAIL WITH GROOVE TRACKS

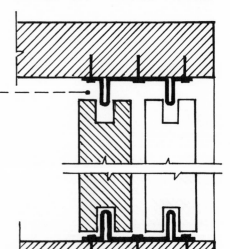

DETAIL WITH METAL TRACKS

SLIDING DOORS

Sliding doors are a solution to the problem of opening and closing cabinet doors where space is limited. Either wooden grooves or metal tracks can be used. Space must generally be left at top for installation and removal of the doors, which should overlap when closed to keep out dust.

STANDARD DRAWER CONSTRUCTION

The construction of drawers is the most difficult operation in furniture building, and standard drawers cannot be constructed without the use of some woodworking machines. The drawer shown here, however, requires only a circular saw to make the grooves for the rabbet joints. The parts are joined with dowels, feather joints and screws, as illustrated.

The best drawer construction is with the dovetail joint—particularly the half-blind dovetail shown on page 26.

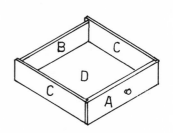

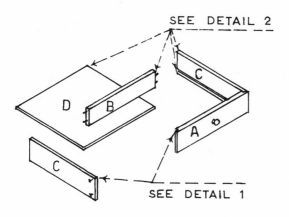

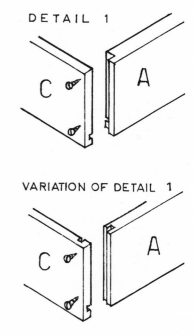

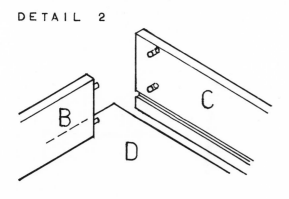

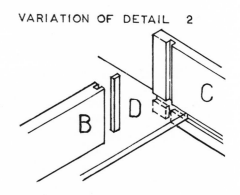

STANDARD DOVETAIL DRAWER CONSTRUCTION

Note: For this construction, add 1 in. length on back (C) to that indicated on List of Materials.

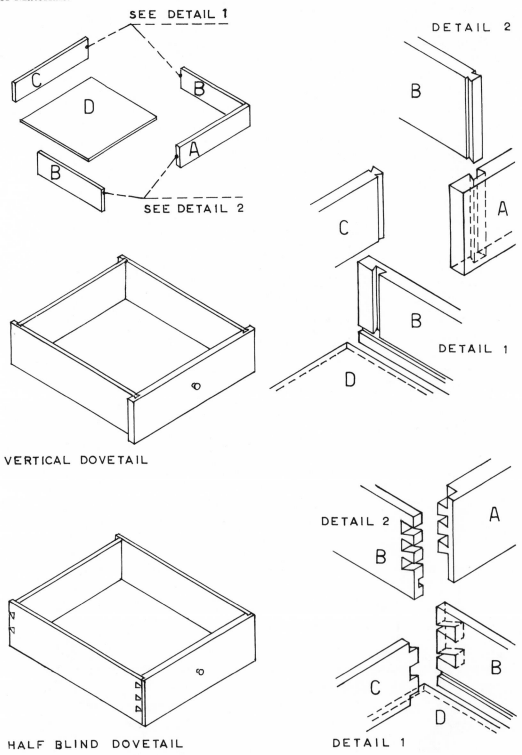

SEE DETAIL 1

DETAIL 2

SEE DETAIL 2

DETAIL 1

VERTICAL DOVETAIL

HALF BLIND DOVETAIL

DETAIL 2

DETAIL 1

SIMPLIFIED DRAWER CONSTRUCTION

Here is a drawer adequate for normal use which can be made by hand. It is designed in the form of a box without cabinet joints, and is assembled with nails. The front is attached with screws driven from the inside, so that the visible portion is unbroken and resembles a standard drawer. A knob or pull can be attached in exactly the same way as for the more complicated type.

Drawer measurements in the lists of materials are intended for standard construc-

tion, but they can easily be adapted to this simplified design. Sides (C) and back (B) are the same for both methods. The simplified front is composed of two parts: (B), which is identical with the back piece, and (A), which is the same length and width as the corresponding piece for a standard drawer, but reduced ⅜ in. in thickness. The bottom (D) will be reduced in width to make it as wide as the back (B), but should be increased from ¼ to ⅜ in. in thickness, to increase the holding power of nails.

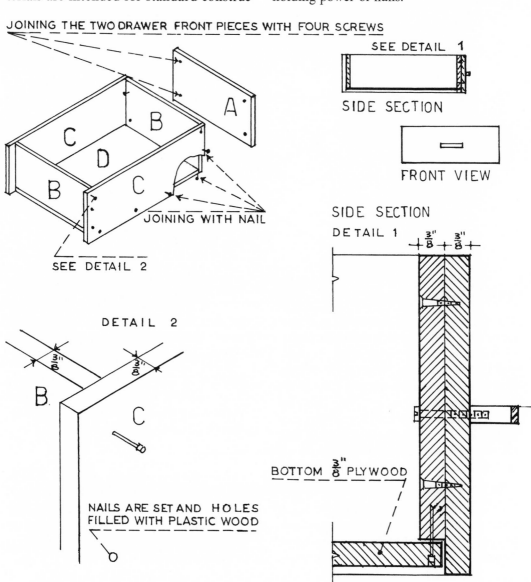

JOINING THE TWO DRAWER FRONT PIECES WITH FOUR SCREWS

SEE DETAIL 1

SIDE SECTION

FRONT VIEW

SIDE SECTION
DETAIL 1

JOINING WITH NAIL

SEE DETAIL 2

DETAIL 2

NAILS ARE SET AND HOLES FILLED WITH PLASTIC WOOD

BOTTOM ⅜" PLYWOOD

INSTRUCTIONS FOR READING DRAWINGS

The drawings used in this book have been especially planned to help the home craftsman visualize the finished piece, its parts, and the way they are fitted together. Each design includes (a) a complete view of the finished piece, (b) front, side, and sectional views as they would appear in a professional cabinet maker's drawings, and (c) an exploded drawing, with parts shown in detail for ordering and cutting. Accompanying instructions give step-by-step procedure for assembly.

Most of the construction details are standard, and are repeated in many different designs. Cross references clearly indicate

the details to be used. Note, however, that letters identifying individual parts refer only to the design in question.

Each set of drawings is accompanied by a list of materials (complete except for minor items of hardware) and a few words suggesting possible applications.

Variations

The designs can be easily varied to fit individual needs by adding or omitting doors, shelves, or units. Decorative moldings may also be added, but it is not advisable for beginners in woodworking to make changes in basic construction.

SECTION 1: BABY FURNITURE

1.1 BASSINET

This basket-bed for infants is easy to make, and easily moved from room to room. The crossed wooden legs fold to permit storage; the mattress, too, can be folded for storage or transport.

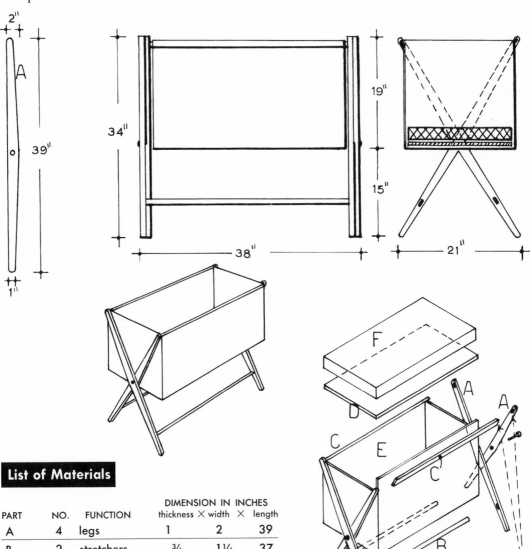

List of Materials

PART	NO.	FUNCTION	DIMENSION IN INCHES thickness × width × length		
			thickness	width	length
A	4	legs	1	2	39
B	2	stretchers	¾	1¼	37
C	2	rails	¾	1¾	37
D	1	plywood panel	⅜	18	33
E	1	plastic sheet		36	80
F	1	foam rubber mattress	3	18	33

Instructions for Assembly

1. Join legs (A) with bolts at center.
2. Fasten stretchers (B) and rails (C) with legs (A).
3. Apply finish.
4. Saw the plastic sheet to indicated shape and attach to rails (C).

DETAIL 1

Bassinet

1.2 CRIB

The fixed side is placed against the wall, while the folding side facilitates making the child's bed or removing the mattress. Double-spring catches make it impossible for inquisitive fingers to unlatch the folding side. Because of the large number of parts that have to be joined, care and accuracy are required in this project.

List of Materials

PART	NO.	FUNCTION	thickness	×	width	×	length
A	4	legs	1		1½		37½
B	2	rails	1		1½		26
C	2	panels	¾		23		28½
D	2	rails	¾		5½		46
E	2	cleats	¾		1		44
F	4	cleats	¾		1		24
G	6	rails	¾		1¼		46
H	2	rails	¾		1¼		24
J	4	rails	¾		1¼		12
K	9	dowels	⅜ diam.				23
L	18	dowels	⅜ diam.				11
M	2	rails	¾		1½		46
O	2	rails	¾		1½		21
P	6	strips	¼		1½		23
Q	1	foam rubber mattress	2		23		45

The dimensions are given under the heading "DIMENSION IN INCHES".

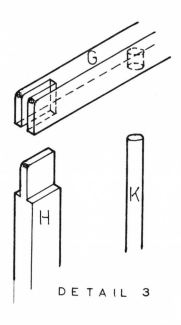

DETAIL 3

Crib

Instructions for Assembly

1. Join legs (A) with panel (C) and rail (B).
2. Attach cleats (E) and (F) to panel (C) and rail (D).
3. Insert dowels (K) in rails (G) and attach rails (H).
4. Insert dowels (L) in rails (G) and attach rails (J) and join rail (G) to hinge.
5. Attach rails (D) and (H) to legs (A) and install the folding side of crib.
6. Join rails (M) and (O) to strip (P).
7. Apply finish.
8. Insert wood frame (M) and (O) and mattress (Q).

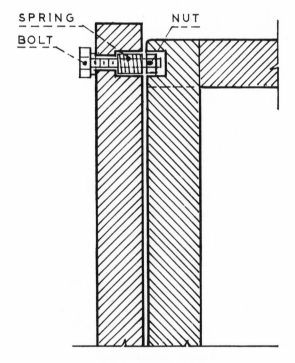

SPRING

NUT

BOLT

SECTION DETAIL 4

DETAIL 4

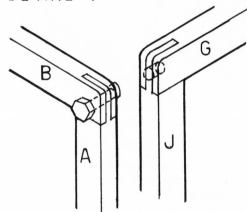

Crib

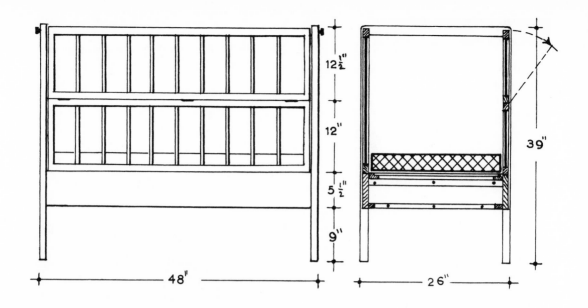

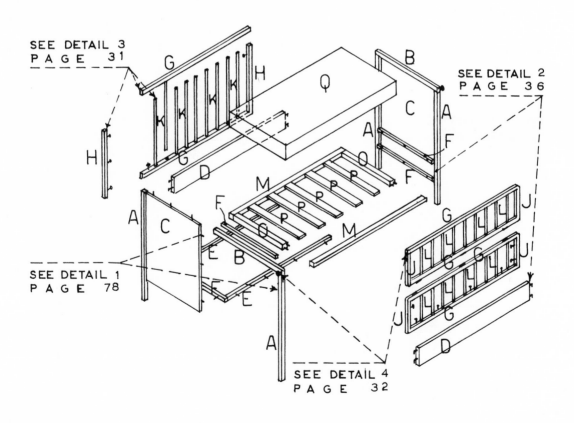

SEE DETAIL 3
PAGE 31

SEE DETAIL 2
PAGE 36

SEE DETAIL 1
PAGE 78

SEE DETAIL 4
PAGE 32

1.3 PORTABLE CRIB

Taking little room space and small enough to be wheeled through a doorway, this crib allows the very young baby to have company while Mother tends to chores in kitchen or utility room.

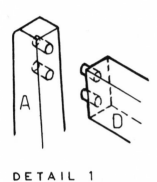

DETAIL 1

List of Materials

PART	NO.	FUNCTION	DIMENSION IN INCHES				
			thickness	×	width	×	length
A	4	legs	1		2½		32½
B	2	rails	¾		5		40
C	2	rails	¾		5		20½
D	2	rails	1		1¼		22
E	8	dowels	⅜ diam.				18
F	4	rails	¾		1¼		17½
G	4	rails	¾		1¼		40
H	14	dowels	⅜ diam.				16½
J	2	cleats	¾		1		40
K	2	cleats	¾		1		20
L	1	plywood panel	⅜		22		40
M	1	foam rubber mattress	3		21		39

1. Install dowels (E) in the rails (C, D) and join rails (C) and (D) with legs (A).
2. Fasten cleats (J) and (K) to rails (B) and (C).
3. Fasten rails (F) and dowels (J) to rails (G) and attach latter to rails (B) with hinge.
4. Fasten rails (B) to legs (A).
5. Apply finish.
6. Insert bottom (L) and mattress (M).

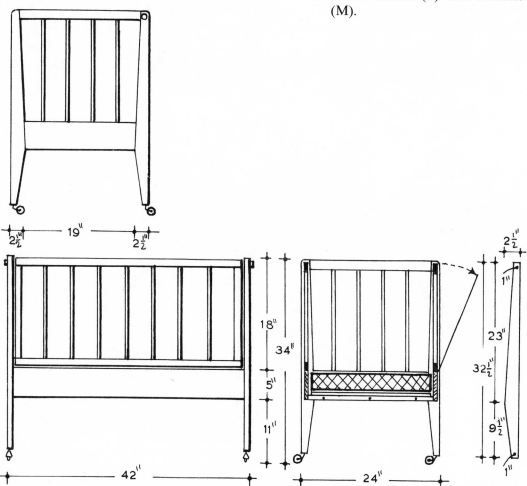

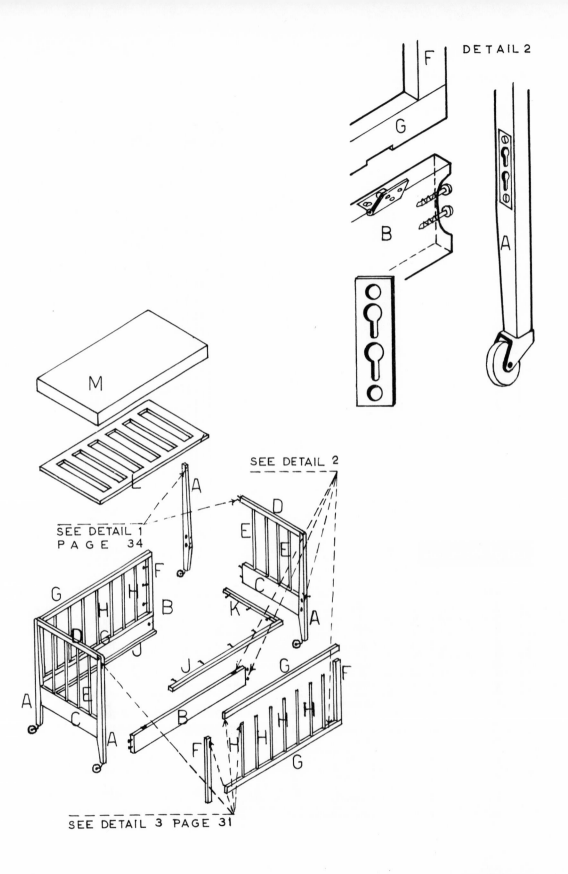

DETAIL 2

SEE DETAIL 2

SEE DETAIL 1
PAGE 34

SEE DETAIL 3 PAGE 31

Portable Crib

1.4 HIGH CHAIR

A broad base and sturdy construction make this model relatively tip-proof. Any kind of finish will do for the chair, but the tray should be enameled to take repeated washing and scrubbing. The time-honored high chair makes junior a joiner at the family table.

List of Materials

PART	NO.	FUNCTION	DIMENSION IN INCHES		
			thickness ×	width ×	length
A	1	back	½	12	13½
B	1	seat	¾	12	13½
C	2	sides	½	5	10
D	4	legs	1¼	1¼	25
E	4	stretchers	⅝ diam.		16
F	4	stretchers	⅝ diam.		13
G	2	braces	½	1	19
H	1	strip	½	1	14½
J	1	panel	½	13½	12
K	1	support	½	4	13
L	1	support	¾	3	13
M	1	strip of leather			9

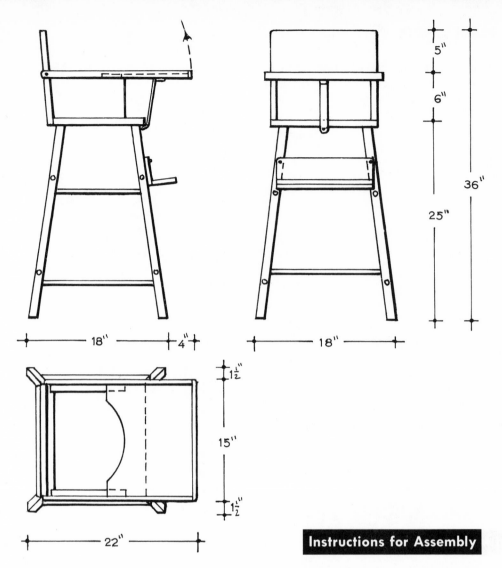

Instructions for Assembly

1. Attach back (A) to seat (B) and to sides (C).
2. Join legs (D) to stretchers (E) and (F).
3. Fasten legs (D) to seat (B).
4. Join strips (G) and (H) to panel (J) and fasten braces (G) to back (A).
5. Join supports (K) and (L) together and fasten to legs (D) with screws.
6. Fasten leather catch (M).
7. Apply finish.

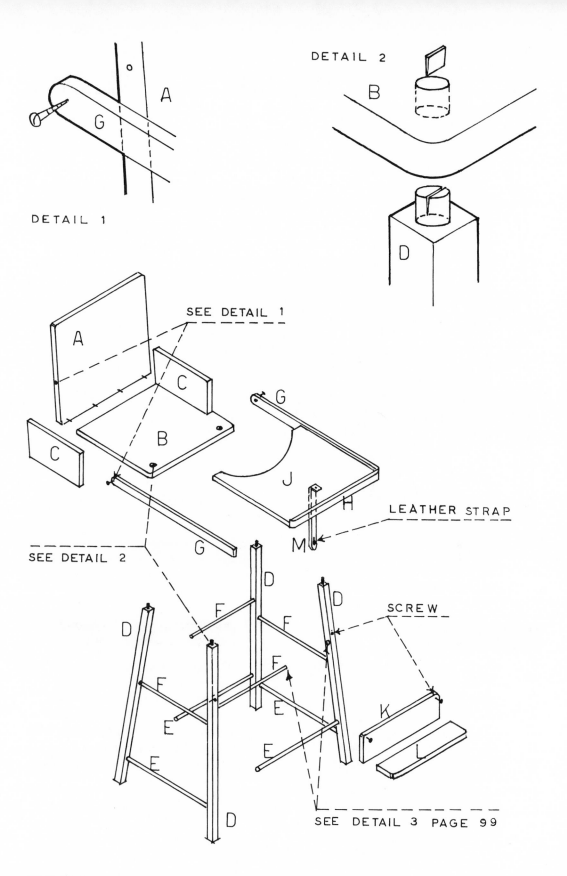

DETAIL 1

DETAIL 2

SEE DETAIL 1

SEE DETAIL 2

LEATHER STRAP

SCREW

SEE DETAIL 3 PAGE 99

1.5 PLAY PEN

This model folds flat for ready portability or storage. Correct placement of the hinges is important for proper folding, as indicated in the plan view. A very useful item if it is not too confining for an active child.

List of Materials

PART	NO.	FUNCTION	DIMENSION IN INCHES thickness × width × length		
A	4	legs	1½	1½	32
B	4	rails	1	1½	37
C	8	rails	1	1½	18½
D	20	dowels	½ diam.		25
E	20	dowels	½ diam.		24
F	2	cleats	⅞	1¼	37
G	2	plywood panels	⅜	19	38
H	2	cleats	¾	2	36

Instructions for Assembly

1. Insert dowels (D) in rails (B) and join rails with legs (A).
2. Fasten cleats (F) to rails (B).
3. Insert dowels (E) in rails (C).
4. Join rails (C) together and with legs (A), using hinges.
5. Join panels (G) together with hinge and attach cleats (H).
6. Apply finish.

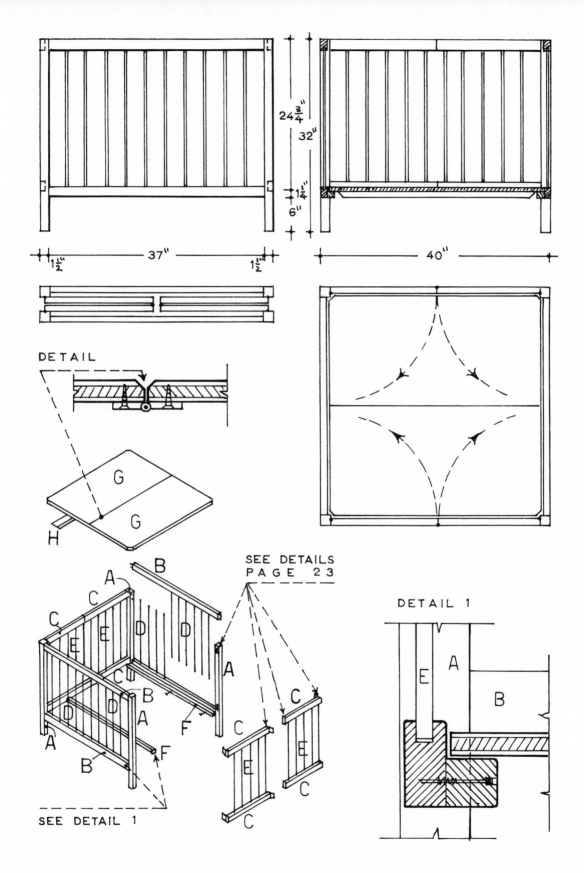

DETAIL

SEE DETAILS
PAGE 23

DETAIL 1

SEE DETAIL 1

SECTION 2: BEDS

2.1 STACKING BEDS

Also called "double-decker" beds or bunks, these can be stacked when the bedroom is small, or used as separate beds when the room is large. The projecting dowels in the bedposts should be rounded so that they can be exposed with safety. The guard rail should be placed at the head of the top bed, permitting a sense of adventure without undue danger.

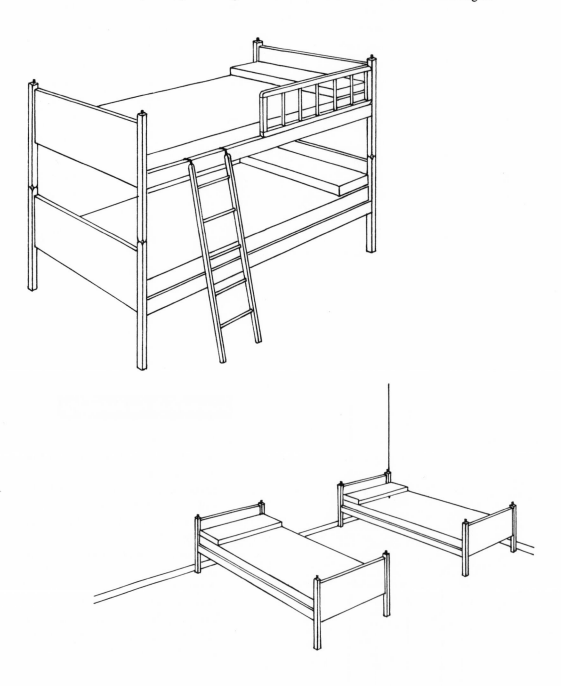

PART	NO.	FUNCTION	DIMENSION IN INCHES		
			thickness ×	width ×	length
A	4	legs	1¾	1¾	32
B	2	panels	¾	18	34½
C	2	side rails	1	5	75
D	2	cleats	1¼	1¼	75
E	2	cleats	1¼	1¼	34½
F	1	plywood panel	½	35½	76½
G	2	rails	¾	1¼	13
H	2	rails	¾	1¼	36
J	5	dowels	⅜ diam.		12
K	5	dowels	¾ diam.		12
L	2	ladder supports	1	1¼	51
M	2	metal catch for ladder			
O	2	rails	¾	2	36½

(for ladder storage in bottom bed)

DETAIL 2

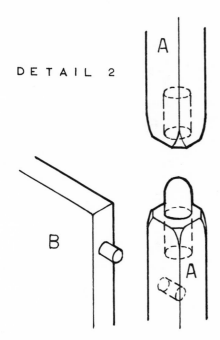

1. Join legs (A) with panel (B).
2. Attach cleats (D) and (E) to rail (C) and panel (B).
3. Insert side (C) in leg (A) and add rail (O) on bottom bed.
4. Insert dowels (J) in rail (H) and attach rails (G).
5. Join dowels (K) to ladder supports (L) and attach metal catch (M).
6. Apply finish.
7. Insert panel (F) and mattress.
8. Place top bed over lower bed and see that dowels on bedposts fit properly.

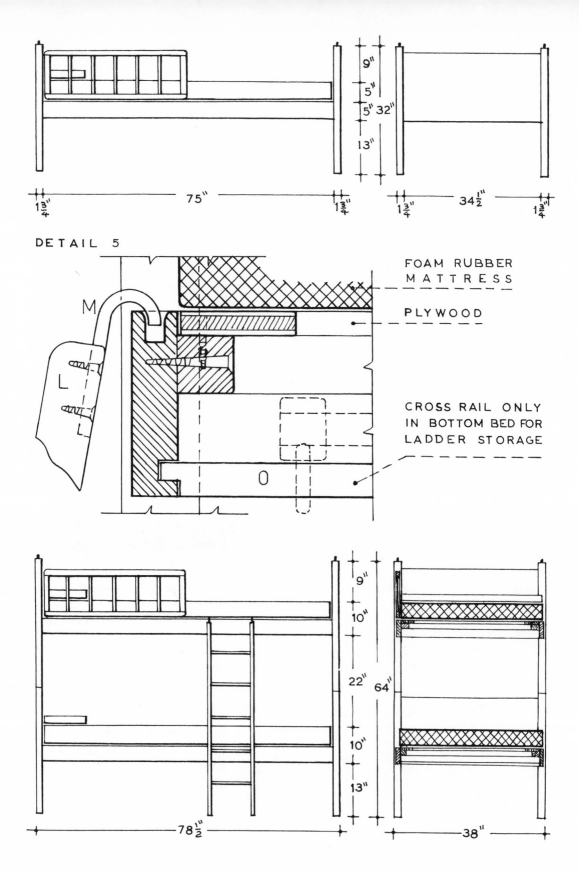

DETAIL 5

FOAM RUBBER
MATTRESS

PLYWOOD

M

CROSS RAIL ONLY
IN BOTTOM BED FOR
LADDER STORAGE

9"

5"

5" 32"

13"

1¾"

75"

1¾"

1¾"

34½"

1¾"

9"

10"

22" 64"

10"

13"

78½"

38"

Stacking Beds

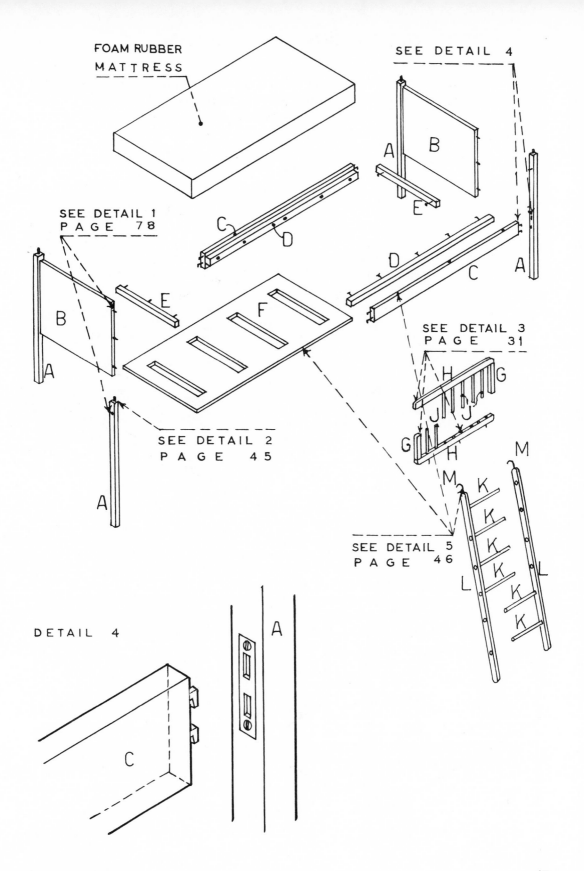

FOAM RUBBER
MATTRESS

SEE DETAIL 4

SEE DETAIL 1
PAGE 78

SEE DETAIL 2
PAGE 45

SEE DETAIL 3
PAGE 31

SEE DETAIL 5
PAGE 46

DETAIL 4

2.2 BUILT-IN DOUBLE DECKER with storage units

No dust under the beds with this neat, space-saving arrangement, and the four drawers provide ample stowage for toys, spare blankets or pajamas. This project requires some degree of craftsmanship and patience, but will provide enormous satisfaction for the whole family. As in Project 2.1, the guard rail should be at the pillow end of the top bed.

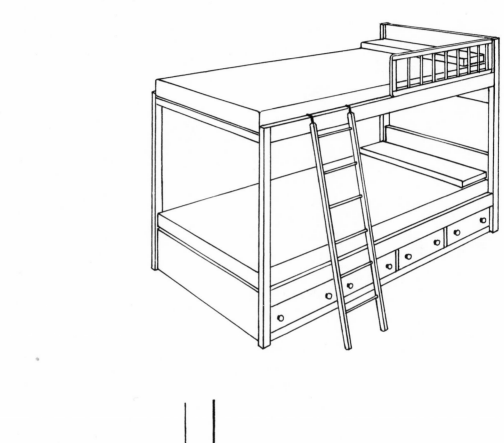

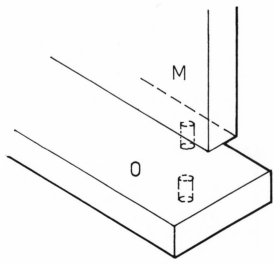

PART	NO.	FUNCTION	DIMENSION IN INCHES		
			thickness ×	width ×	length
A	2	supports	1½	2½	64
B	2	supports	1½	2½	54
C	4	rails	1½	4	73
D	1	headboard	¾	17	36
E	1	headboard	¾	24	36
F	1	rail	1½	2½	36
G	1	panel	¾	13	36
H	4	cleats	1¼	1½	75
J	3	cleats	1¼	1½	33½
K	1	back	¾	9	73
L	1	plywood panel	⅜	36	73
M	3	partitions	1	8	37
O	5	drawer slides	¾	3	36½
P	1	toeplate	1	2	73
Q	2	rails	¾	1¼	36
R	2	rails	¾	1¼	9½
S	7	dowels	⅜ diam.		8½
T	2	rails	1	1½	55
U	6	dowels	⅞ diam.		12
V	4	drawer fronts	¾	7	17½
W	8	drawer sides	½	7	36¾
X	4	drawer backs	½	6½	16½
Y	4	drawer bottoms	¼	17	36½
Z	50 ft	rubber straps	2″ wide		

Instructions for Assembly

1. Join supports (A) with headboards (D) and (E) and supports (B) with rail (F) and panel (G).
2. Fasten supports (A) and (B) with rails (C), back (K) and toeplate (P).
3. Attach partition (M) to drawer slides (O) and fasten to rails (C), back (K) and toeplate (P).
4. Attach cleats (H) to rail (C) and cleats (J) to headboards (D) and (E) and to panel (G).
5. Install plywood panel (L) and rubber strap (Z) as shown in detail drawing.
6. Insert dowels (S) in rails (Q) and attach rails (R).
7. Join sides of drawers (W) to front (V) and back (X); install bottoms (Y).
8. Join dowels (U) with ladder supports (T).
9. Apply finish.

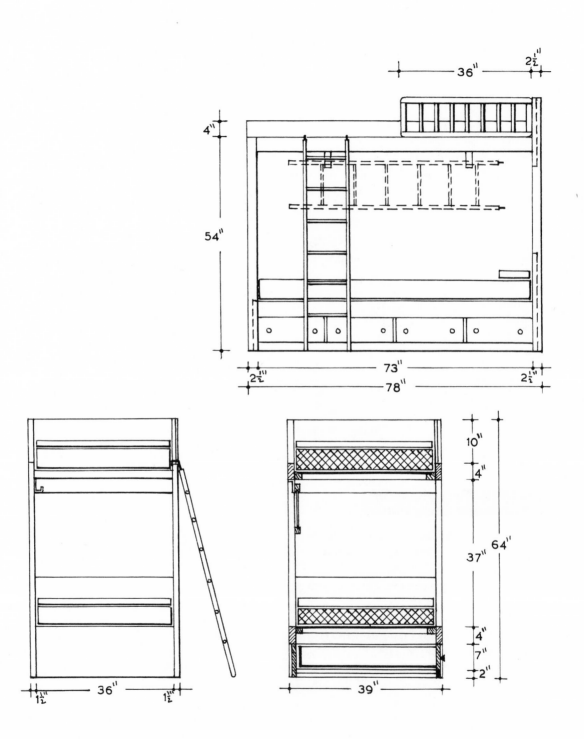

Built-in Double Decker with Storage Units

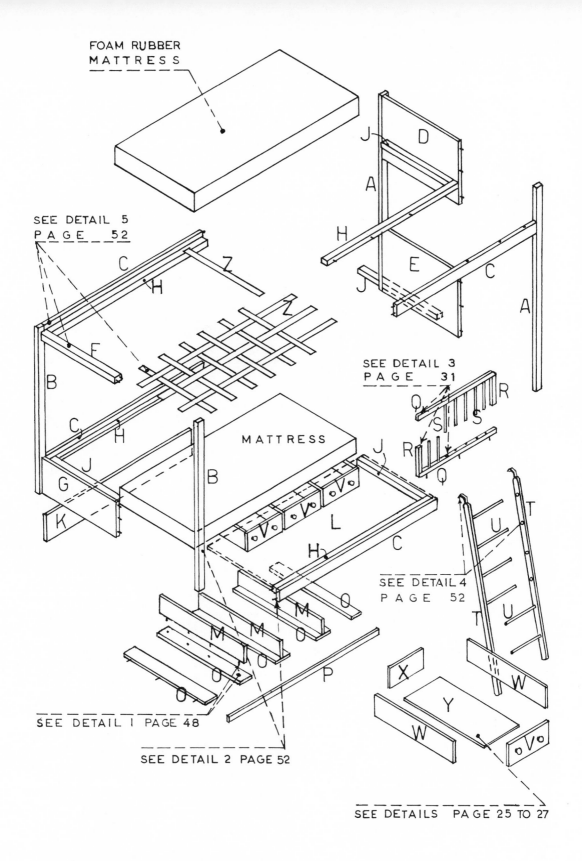

FOAM RUBBER
MATTRESS

SEE DETAIL 5
PAGE 52

SEE DETAIL 3
PAGE 31

MATTRESS

SEE DETAIL 4
PAGE 52

SEE DETAIL 1 PAGE 48

SEE DETAIL 2 PAGE 52

SEE DETAILS PAGE 25 TO 27

Built-in Double Decker with Storage Units   **51**

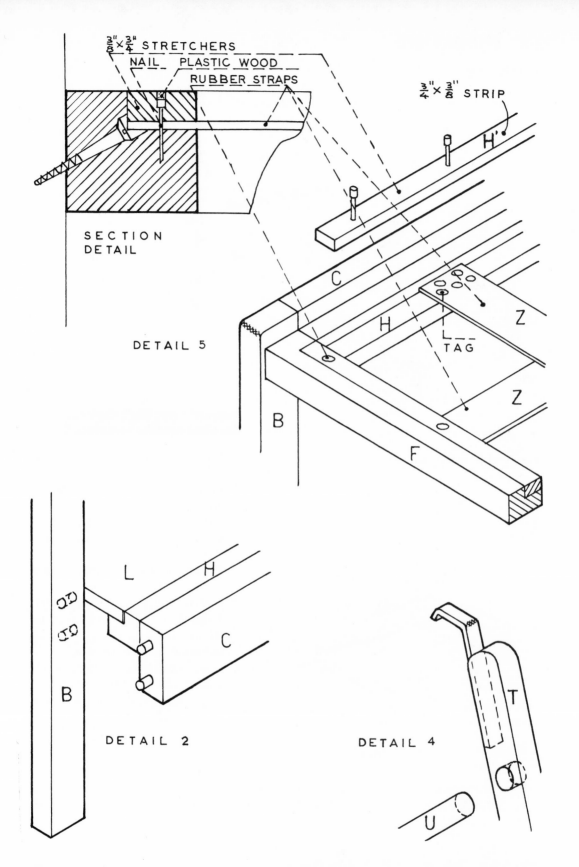

$\frac{3}{8}'' \times \frac{3}{4}''$ STRETCHERS

NAIL   PLASTIC WOOD

RUBBER STRAPS

$\frac{3}{4}'' \times \frac{3}{8}''$ STRIP

H'

SECTION
DETAIL

DETAIL 5

C

H

Z

TAG

Z

B

F

L

H

C

B

DETAIL 2

T

DETAIL 4

U

Built-in Double Decker with Storage Units

2.3 TRUNDLE BED

A modern version of the classic bedroom space-saver. The legs of the main or upper bed can be made shorter if desired, provided the trundle bed is not made up with pillow. This is a highly practical solution when the bedroom is small and play space is scarce.

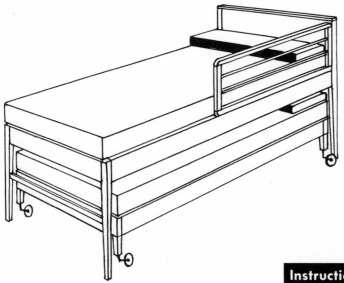

Instructions for Assembly

1. Join legs (A) with rails (E) and (F), and legs (B) with headboard (C).
2. Fasten side rails (G) to legs (A) and (B).
3. Attach strip (D) and cleats (H, J) to headboard (C) and rails (E) and (G).
4. Proceed in same manner for lower bed.
5. Fasten rubber straps to cleats (H, J and R) with tags and cover the straps with strips (K, L and S) as indicated in detail drawing.
6. Insert stretchers (N) in rails (O) and attach rails (M).
7. Apply finish and insert casters in trundle bed.

List of Materials

PART	NO.	FUNCTION	DIMENSION IN INCHES		
			thickness ×	width ×	length
A	2	legs	1½	1½	23
B	2	legs	1½	1½	36
C	1	headboard	¾	16½	36
D	1	strip	½	1½	39
E	3	rails	1	4	36
F	2	rails	¾	1¼	38
G	2	side rails	1	4	74
H	4	cleats	¾	¾	37
J	2	cleats	¾	¾	75
K	2	strips	⅜	¾	75
L	4	strips	⅜	¾	37
M	2	rails	¾	1¼	36
N	2	stretchers	⅜	1	35
O	2	rails	¾	1¼	12½
P	4	legs	1½	1½	10
Q	2	side rails	1	4	70
R	2	cleats	¾	¾	71
S	2	strips	⅜	¾	71
T	100 ft	rubber straps	2″ wide		

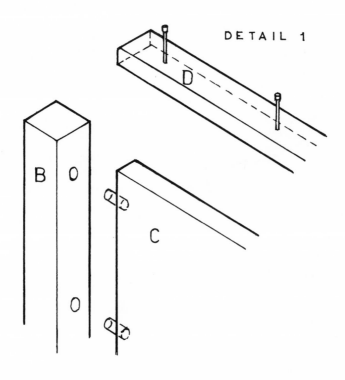

DETAIL 1

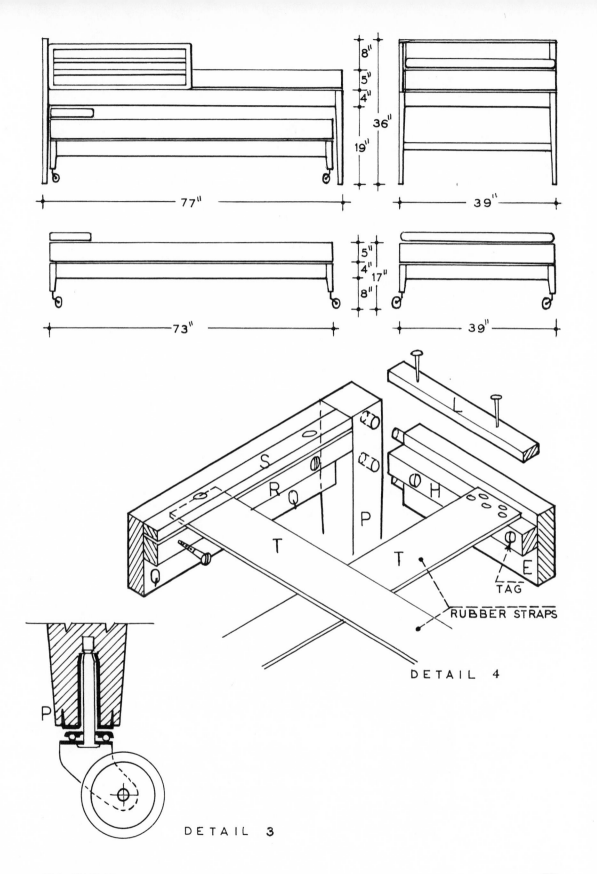

DETAIL 4

DETAIL 3

RUBBER STRAPS

Trundle Bed

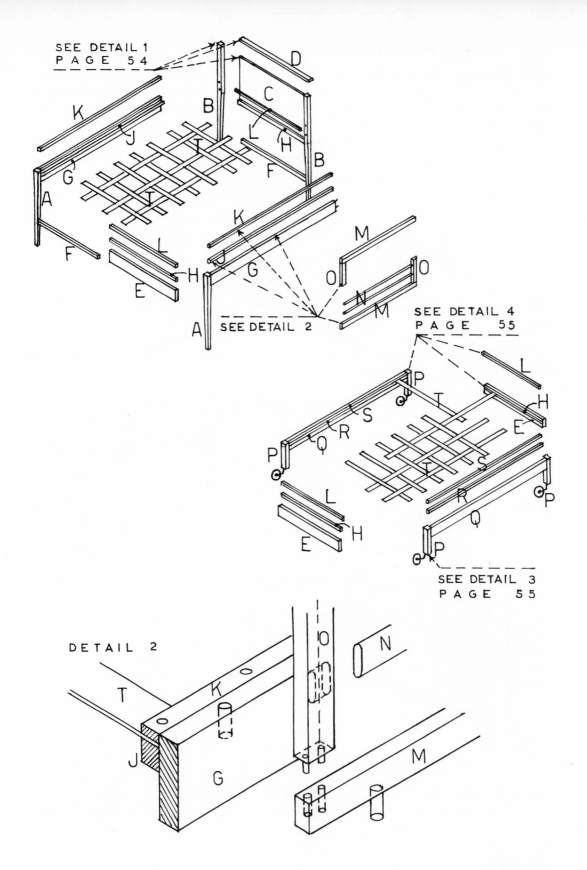

SEE DETAIL 1
P A G E 5 4

SEE DETAIL 2

SEE DETAIL 4
P A G E 5 5

SEE DETAIL 3
P A G E 5 5

DETAIL 2

Trundle Bed

2.4 JUNIOR BED WITH HEADBOARD

An interesting and practical piece that provides desk and storage space without being cumbersome. The bed matches any one of the four designs of headboard. In variations A and B the angle of the sliding doors permits a shut-in to be supported by pillows while reading or drawing.

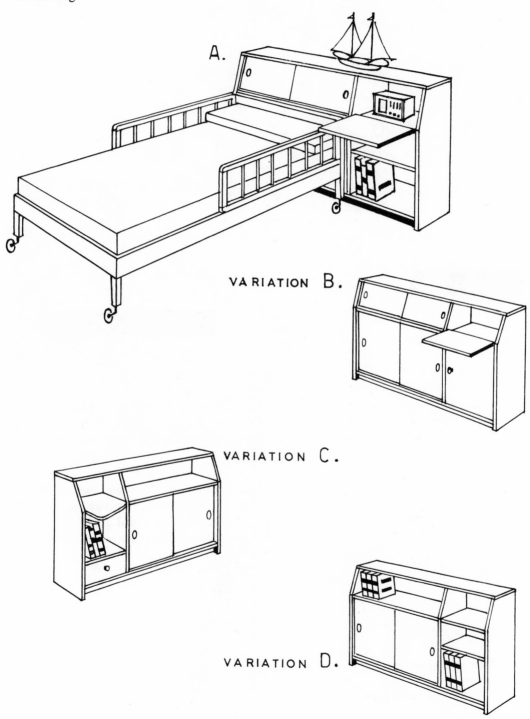

A.

VARIATION B.

VARIATION C.

VARIATION D.

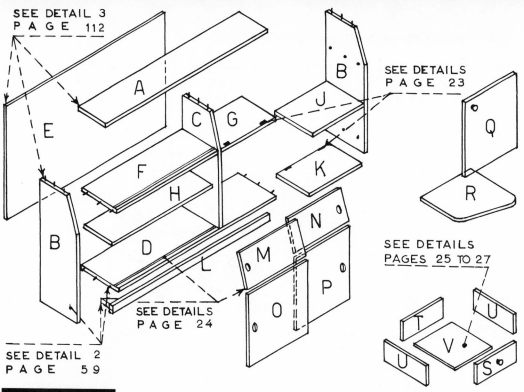

SEE DETAIL 3
PAGE 112

SEE DETAILS
PAGE 23

SEE DETAILS
PAGES 25 TO 27

SEE DETAILS
PAGE 24

SEE DETAIL 2
PAGE 59

List of Materials

Headboards A and B

PART	NO.	FUNCTION	thickness	× width	× length
A	1	top	¾	8¼	66
B	2	sides	¾	12	38¼
C	1	partition	¾	11¾	34½
D	1	bottom	¾	12	64½
E	1	back	¼	35½	65½
F	1	shelf	¾	11¾	40½
G	1	shelf	¾	11¾	23¼
H	1	shelf	¾	10	40½
J	1	shelf	½	11¾	23¼
K	1	door	¾	13	23¼
L	1	toeplate	¾	3	64½
M	1	door	¼	13¼	20¼
N	1	door	¼	13¼	21¼
O	1	door	¼	22¼	20¼
P	1	door	¼	22¼	21¼

The headers **DIMENSION IN INCHES** span the last three columns: thickness × width × length.

Variation for Headboard B

| Q | 1 | door | ¾ | 23¼ | 21¾ |

Also reduce shelf (J) above to 10 in. width.

Headboards C and D

Reduce length by 6 in.; eliminate all top doors. Shelves
G and J are 17¼ in. in length.

Variation for Headboard C

R	1	shelf	¾	17¼	18
S	1	drawer front	¾	6	17¼
T	1	drawer back	½	5½	16¼
U	2	drawer sides	½	6	11⅜
V	1	drawer bottom	¼	16¾	11¼

Instructions for Assembly

1. Join bottom (D) and shelves (F) and (G) with partition (C) and side (B).
2. Attach top (A) and back (E).
3. Fasten toeplate (L) and door (K).
4. Install shelves (H) and (J) and add doors (M, N, O and P).
5. Apply finish.
6. If variations are used, add door (Q); build drawer and join side (U) with front and backs (S) and (T), and install drawer bottom (V).

Junior Bed with Headboard

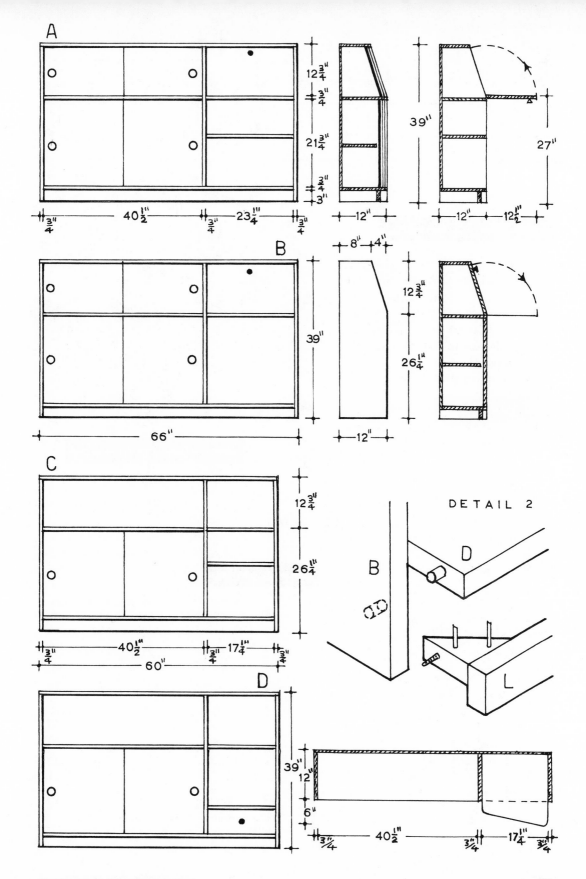

Junior Bed with Headboard

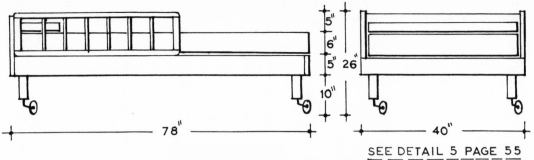

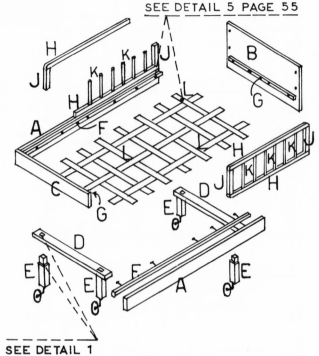

SEE DETAIL 5 PAGE 55

SEE DETAIL 1

Instructions for Assembly

1. Join crossrails (D) with legs (E).
2. Fasten side rail (A) to rails (D) and (C) and headboard (B).
3. Attach strips (F) and (G) to rails (A) and (C) and headboard (B).
4. Insert dowels in rails (H) and attach rails (J).
5. Fasten rubber strip (L) to strips (F) and (G).
6. Apply finish.
7. Insert casters, install mattress and side protection.

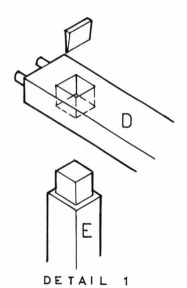

DETAIL 1

List of Materials — BED

PART	NO.	FUNCTION	DIMENSION IN INCHES		
			thickness ×	width ×	length
A	2	side rails	1	5	76
B	1	board	¾	15	40
C	1	rail	1	5	40
D	2	rails	1	2	38
E	4	legs	1⅜	1⅜	8
F	2	strips	¾	1	76
G	2	strips	¾	1¼	36
H	4	rails	¾	1¼	42
J	4	rails	¾	1¼	11
K	12	dowels	⅜ diam.		10
L	50	rubber strips	2″ wide		

2.5 BED TRAY

Besides the obvious mealtime uses for the convalescent child, this bed tray also doubles as a play table, the raised edge keeping pencils and crayons from rolling onto the floor. The legs fold in flat for closet storage.

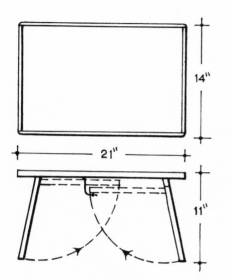

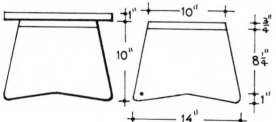

List of Materials

PART	NO.	FUNCTION	DIMENSION IN INCHES thickness × width × length		
A	1	top	¾	13¼	20¼
B	2	strips	⅜	1	21
C	2	strips	⅜	1	13¼
D	1	support	¾	10	14
E	1	support	¾	9¼	14
F	1	strip	¾	¾	10½

Instructions for Assembly

1. Attach strips (B) and (C) to top (A).
2. Fasten strip (F) to top (A).
3. Join supports (D) and (E) to top (A) and strip (F).
4. Install leather catch on top (reverse side).
5. Apply finish.

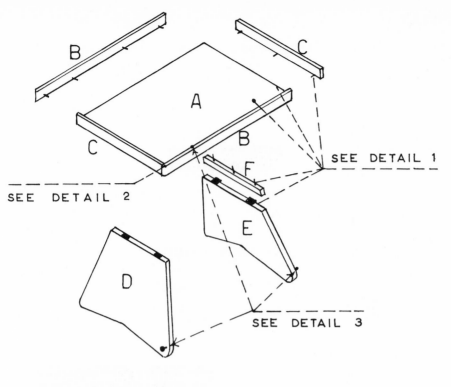

B

C

A

B

SEE DETAIL 1

F

SEE DETAIL 2

E

D

SEE DETAIL 3

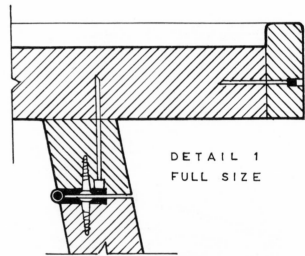

DETAIL 1
FULL SIZE

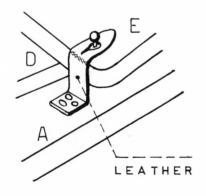

DETAIL 3
UNDERSIDE OF TRAY

D

E

A

LEATHER

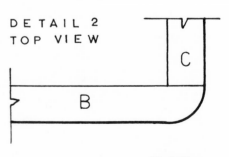

DETAIL 2
TOP VIEW

C

B

Bed Tray

SECTION 3: ROOM IMPROVERS

3.1 RADIATOR ENCLOSURE

Besides its aesthetic value, this radiator cover protects young children from bruises and burns, and the bottom rail prevents marbles and other small objects from rolling under the radiator. Dimensions are adaptable to size of radiator.

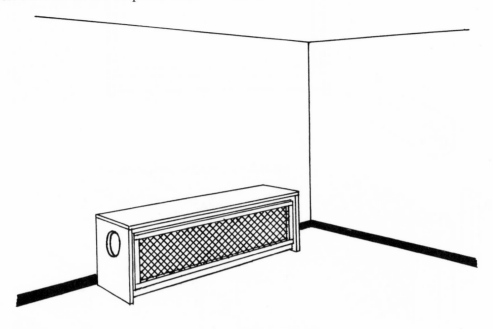

VARIATION IN SIZE

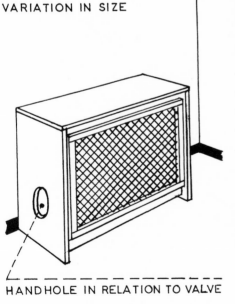

HANDHOLE IN RELATION TO VALVE

List of Materials

PART	NO.	FUNCTION	DIMENSION IN INCHES thickness × width × length		
A	1	top	¾	W	D
B	2	sides	¾	H	D
C	2	rails	1	2	W less 1½
D	2	rails	¾	1¼	W less 2½
E	2	rails	¾	1¼	H less 6½
F	1	sheet of expanded metal	H less 6 in.		W less 3 in.

Instructions for Assembly

1. Join side (B) with rail (C) and attach top (A).
2. Fasten rails (D) to (E) and attach metal sheet (F).
3. Join rail (D) to rail (C) and apply finish.
4. Install enclosure over radiator.

Radiator Enclosure

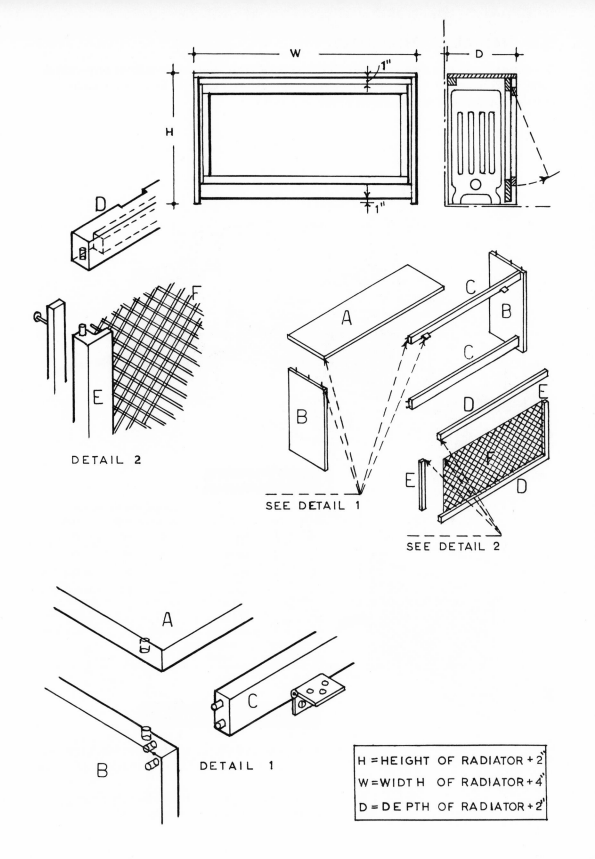

W

H

1"

1"

D

D

D

F

E

DETAIL 2

A

C

B

C

B

D

E

E

F

D

SEE DETAIL 1

SEE DETAIL 2

A

C

B

DETAIL 1

H = HEIGHT OF RADIATOR + 2"
W = WIDTH OF RADIATOR + 4"
D = DEPTH OF RADIATOR + 2"

Radiator Enclosure

3.2 MODULAR BOOKCASE

An original and practical unit that adds a note of vivacity to any room. Groups can be built up as desired, with or without the central shelf. You can add as many "modules" as you wish, either vertically or horizontally.

List of Materials

PART	NO.	FUNCTION	DIMENSION IN INCHES		
			thickness ×	width ×	length
		Design No. 1			
A	1	back	¼	36	36
B	2	pieces	¾	11¾	36
C	4	pieces	¾	11¾	12
D	4	pieces	¾	11¾	10½
		Design No. 2			
A	1	back	¼	36	36
B	4	pieces	¾	11¾	12¾
C	4	pieces	¾	11¾	12
D	4	pieces	¾	11¾	10½

Instructions for Assembly

(Both Designs)

1. Join piece (B) with piece (C).
2. Fasten piece (D) to piece (C) and (C) with piece (B).
3. Install back (A).
4. Apply finish.

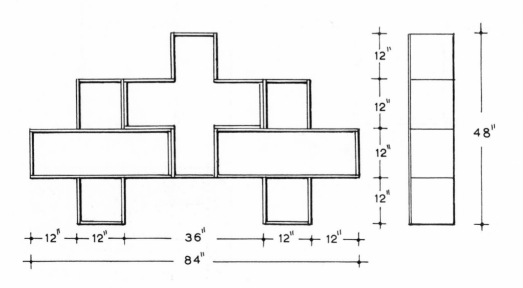

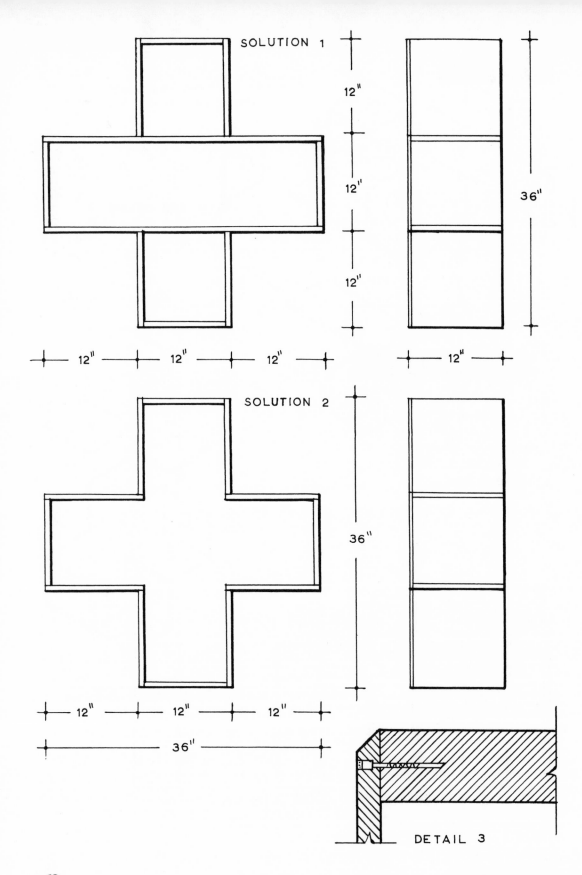

SOLUTION 1

12"

12"

12"

36"

12" · 12" · 12"

12"

SOLUTION 2

36"

12" · 12" · 12"

36"

12"

DETAIL 3

Modular Bookcase

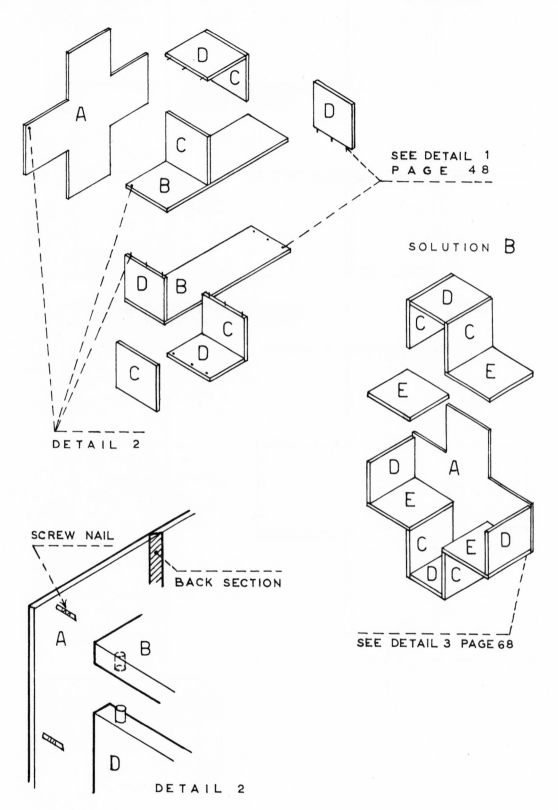

SOLUTION A

D

C

A

D

C

B

D

SEE DETAIL 1
PAGE 48

SOLUTION B

D

B

D

C

C

D

DETAIL 2

C

D

C

C

E

E

E

D

A

E

C

E

D

D

C

SEE DETAIL 3 PAGE 68

SCREW NAIL

BACK SECTION

A

B

D

DETAIL 2

3.3 CLOTHES TREE

How can we train young ones to hang up their clothes if they can't reach the closet rack? This child-size clothes tree makes it fun to hang things up—and take them down. The top shelf holds school books, games or assorted pieces of play equipment.

List of Materials

PART	NO.	FUNCTION	DIMENSION IN INCHES thickness × width × length		
A	1	top	¾ × 18 in. diam.		
B	1	support	1½	1½	45
C	4	legs	1	2½	10
D	2	dowels	¾ diam.		22
E	2	hangers	¾	1½	14
F	2	hangers	¾ × 2 in. diam.		
G	4	hook	½ diam.		5

Instructions for Assembly

1. Join support (B) with legs (C).
2. Insert dowels (D) in support (B) and attach hangers (E) and (F) to dowels (D).
3. Install top (A) and hook (G) to support (B).
4. Apply finish.

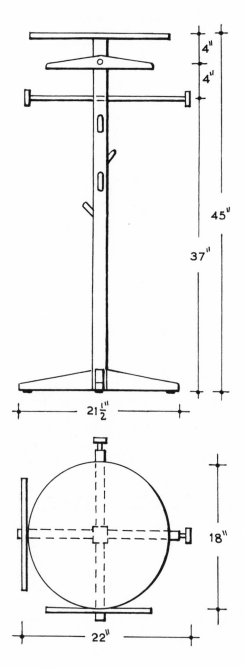

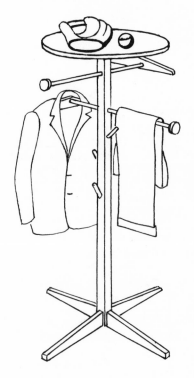

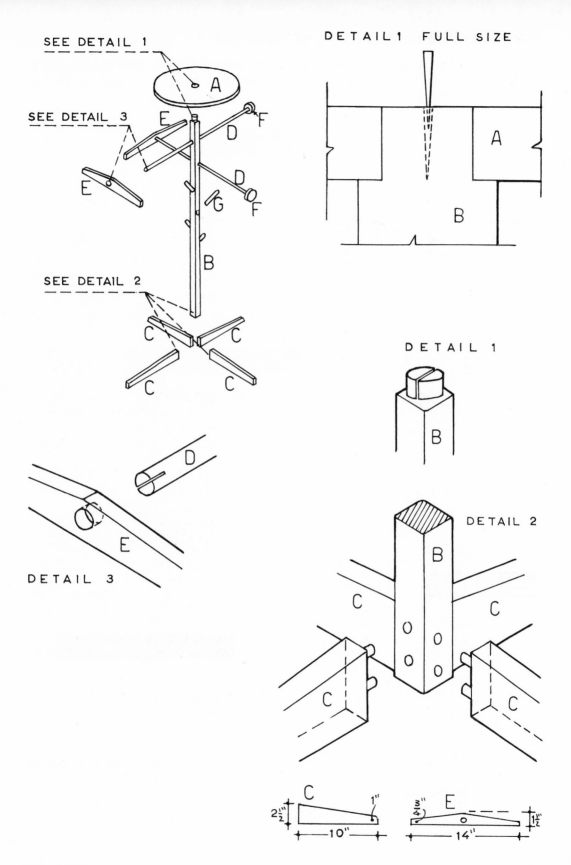

SEE DETAIL 1

SEE DETAIL 3

SEE DETAIL 2

DETAIL 1 FULL SIZE

DETAIL 1

DETAIL 2

DETAIL 3

Clothes Tree

3.4   BULLETIN BOARD OR CHALKBOARD

Both are useful all the way from preschool to high school. For a bulletin board, use soft wallboard to take thumbtacks. For a chalkboard, add the lower ledge and use hard-surfaced Masonite covered by green chalkboard paint.

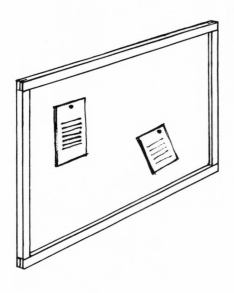

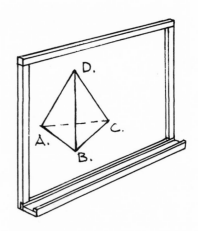

List of Materials

Bulletin Board

PART	NO.	FUNCTION	thickness	× width	× length
			DIMENSION IN INCHES		
A	2	rails	¾	1¼	30
B	2	rails	¾	1¼	21
C	1	wallboard or cork panel	³⁄₁₆	19½	28½
D	1	plywood panel	¼	19½	28½

Chalkboard

PART	NO.	FUNCTION	thickness	× width	× length
A	2	rails	¾	1¼	24
B	2	rails	¼	1¼	18
C	1	Masonite panel	¼	16½	22½
E	1	board	¾	⅜	24

Instructions for Assembly

1. Join rails (A) with rails (B).
2. Install wallboard or cork (C) with plywood back (D) for bulletin board.
3. Apply finish.
4. For chalkboard, install the Masonite in place of the wallboard or cork, and paint with green chalkboard paint.

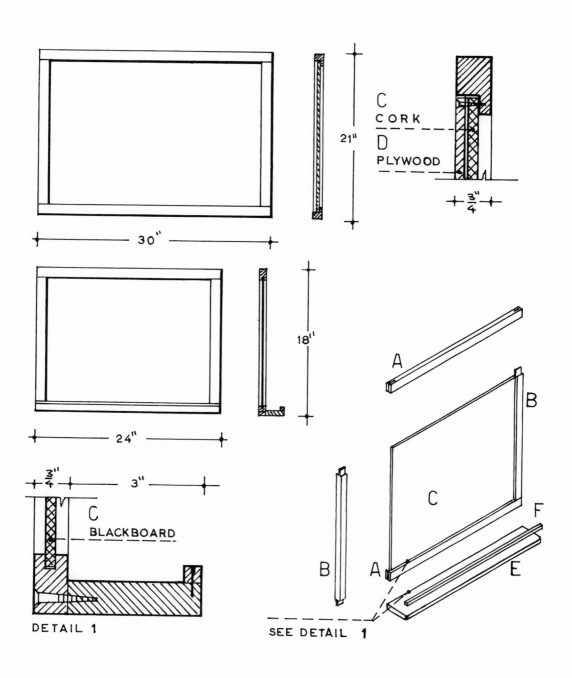

21"

C
CORK
D
PLYWOOD

3/4"

30"

18"

24"

A

B

C

F

B

A

E

3/4"   3"

C
BLACKBOARD

DETAIL 1

SEE DETAIL 1

3.5 DISPLAY TREE

Ideal for mounting collections of leaves, butterflies and other nature objects, as well as maps, charts and artwork. Both sides of each "leaf" can be used, and each leaf is demountable. For dust protection, cover with transparent plastic.

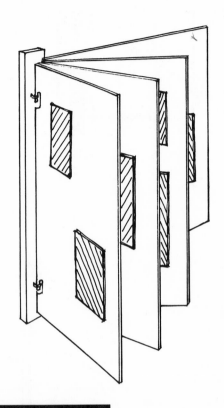

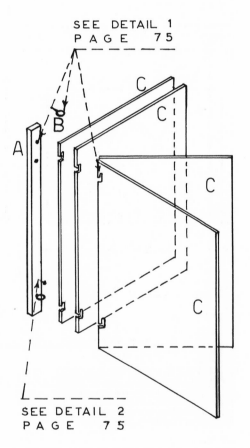

SEE DETAIL 1
PAGE 75

SEE DETAIL 2
PAGE 75

List of Materials

PART	NO.	FUNCTION	DIMENSION IN INCHES thickness × width × length		
A	1	support	1	4	39
B	2	screws with ring head			
C	4	Masonite panels	¼	30	36

Instructions for Assembly

1. Attach ring-head screws (B) to wood support (A).
2. Apply finish.
3. Fasten wood support (A) to wall with "molly" bolts (self-anchoring).
4. Install panel (C).

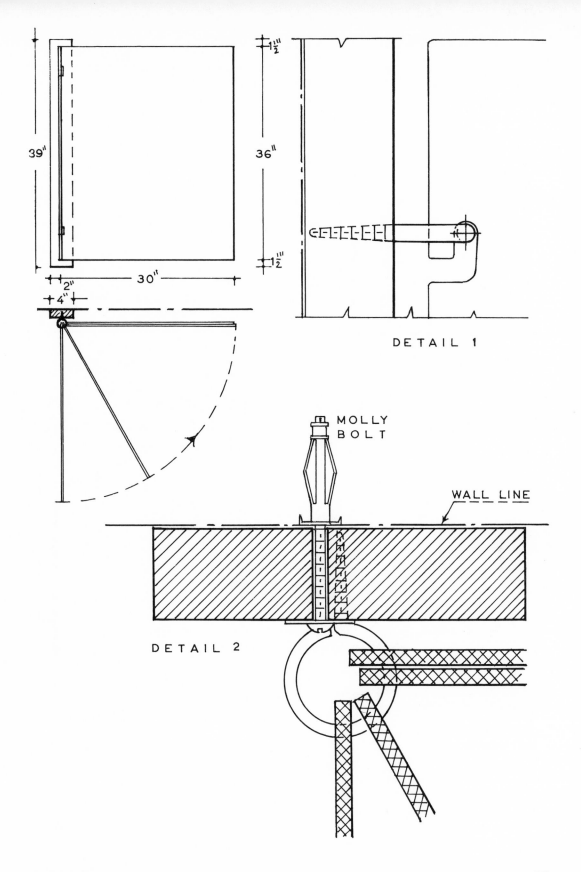

39"

36"

$1\frac{1}{2}$"

$1\frac{1}{2}$"

30"

2"

4"

DETAIL 1

MOLLY
BOLT

WALL LINE

DETAIL 2

SECTION 4: TABLES, DESKS AND CHAIRS

4.1 KNEEHOLE DESK

Not too difficult to make yet good-looking, sturdy and practical for any room in the house. Note the left-hand well for magazines and outsize books. Instead of paint or lacquer many do-it-yourselfers use "contact" plastic covering, which can be had in a variety of wood grains and colors.

List of Materials

PART	NO.	FUNCTION	DIMENSION IN INCHES thickness × width × length		
A	1	top	¾	22	42
B	1	rail	¾	4	18
C	1	rail	¾	4	23
D	4	legs	1¼	1½	27¼
E	2	sides	¾	19¾	19½
F	2	pieces	¾	19	14½
G	1	back	¾	14½	19½
H	8	cleats	⅜	½	19
J	1	rail	¾	2	23
K	3	drawer fronts	¾	6	14½
L	6	drawer sides	½	6	18⅝
M	3	drawer backs	½	5½	13½
O	3	drawer bottoms	¼	14	18½
P	1	drawer front	¾	3¼	23
Q	1	drawer back	½	2¾	22
R	2	drawer sides	½	3¼	18⅝
S	1	drawer bottom	¼	22½	18½
T	2	sides	½	5½	12
U	1	back	½	12	18
V	1	front	½	11	18
W	1	bottom	½	2	17

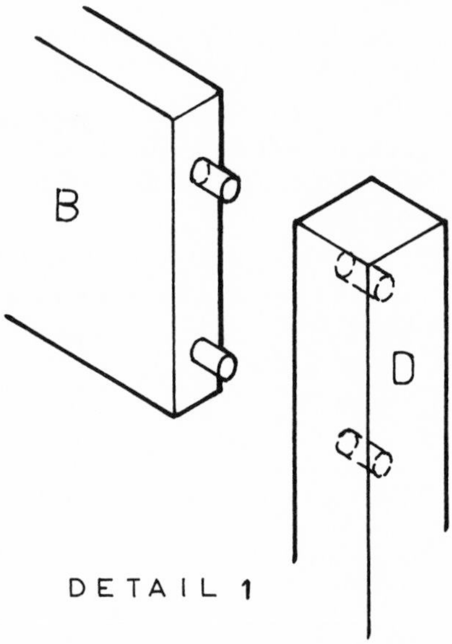

DETAIL 1

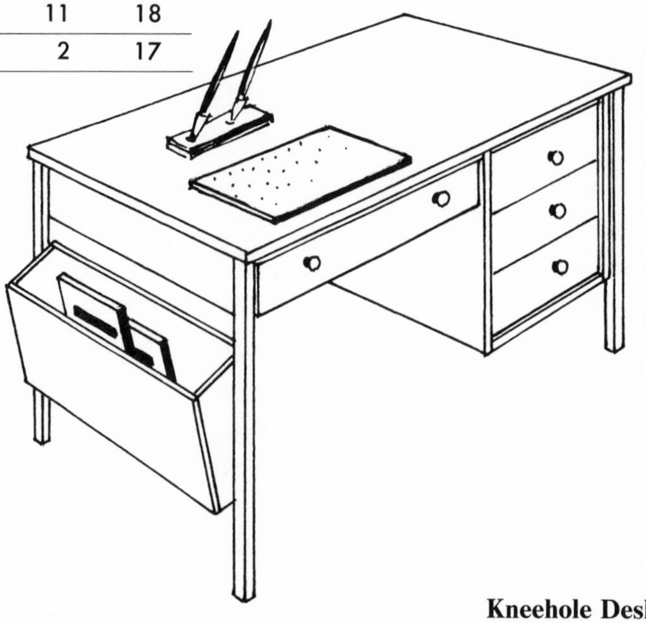

1. Fasten pieces (F) with sides (E) and back (G).
2. Join legs (D) with rails (B) and (C) and with sides (E) and rails (J).
3. Fasten top (A) to frame thus formed.
4. Attach cleats (H) to rail (B) and sides (E).
5. Join drawer side (L) with drawer front (K) and back (M), and install drawer bottom (O).
6. Join drawer sides (R) with fronts (P) and back (Q) and install bottom (S).
7. Fasten back (U) to bottom (W), sides (T), front (V) and attach to legs (D).
8. Apply finish.

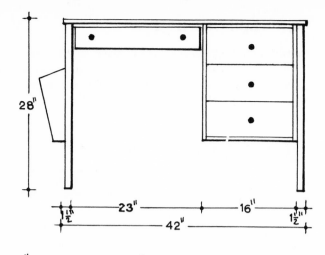

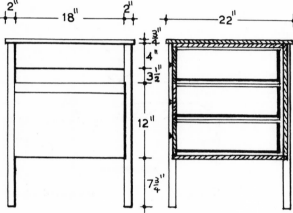

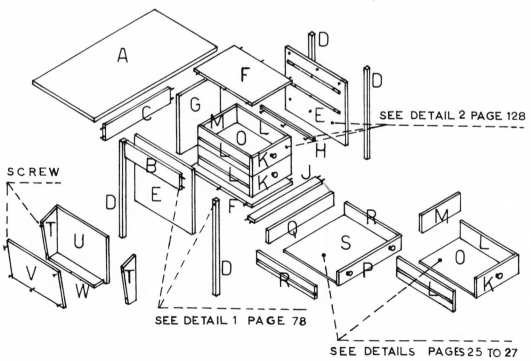

SEE DETAIL 2 PAGE 128

SCREW

SEE DETAIL 1 PAGE 78

SEE DETAILS PAGES 25 TO 27

Kneehole Desk

79

4.2 BUILT-IN DESK

Besides making full use of the space between two closets, this design provides extra work space for drawing—or play space for games. Teen-agers with lots of books and papers for "research" assignments will appreciate the larger working surface. A wall-to-wall bulletin board over the desk or a large map will be both esthetic and functional.

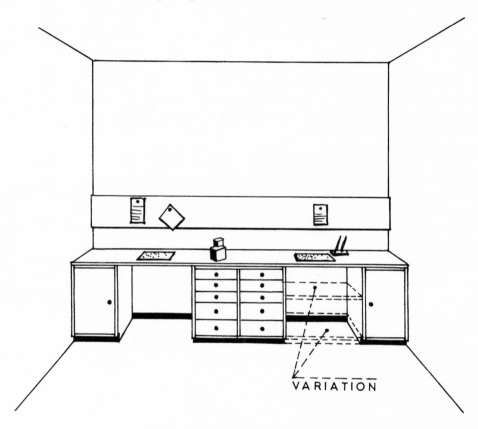

VARIATION

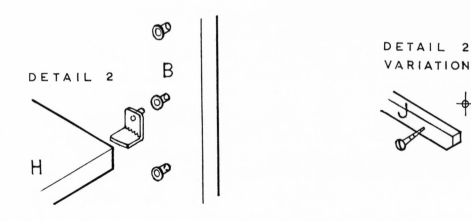

DETAIL 2

B

H

DETAIL 2
VARIATION

B

List of Materials

PART	NO.	FUNCTION	DIMENSION IN INCHES		
			thickness ×	width ×	length
A	1	top	1	18	W
B	6	sides	¾	17	27
B	1	partition	¾	16¾	24
C	8	tops and bottoms	¾	14½	17
D	4	backs	¼	15½	23½
E	2	doors	¾	14½	22½
F	2	bases	¾	3	14½
G	1	base	¾	3	29¾
H	2	shelves	¾	14½	15
J	20	cleats	⅜	¾	14
K	6	drawer fronts	¾	3½	14½
L	6	drawer backs	½	3	13½
M	12	drawer sides	½	3½	16⅜
O	10	drawer bottoms	¼	14	16¼
P	4	drawer fronts	¾	6	14½
Q	4	drawer backs	½	5½	13½
R	8	drawer sides	½	6	16⅜
T	2	add'l shelves	¾	16¾	W^2
U	1	toe plate	¾	3	W^2

Instructions for Assembly

1. Join sides (B) with tops and bottoms (C).
2. Install backs (D).
3. Fasten toeplate or bases (F) and (G) to sides (B) and bottoms (C).
4. Attach cleats (J) to sides (B) and install doors (E) and shelves (H).
5. Join drawer sides (M) to drawer fronts (K) and backs (L) and install drawer bottoms (O).
6. Join drawer sides (R) to drawer fronts (P) and backs (Q) and install drawer bottoms (O).
7. Apply finish.
8. Set cabinet in place and fasten top (A).
9. Add shelves (T) and toeplate (U) if variation is desired.

Built-in Desk

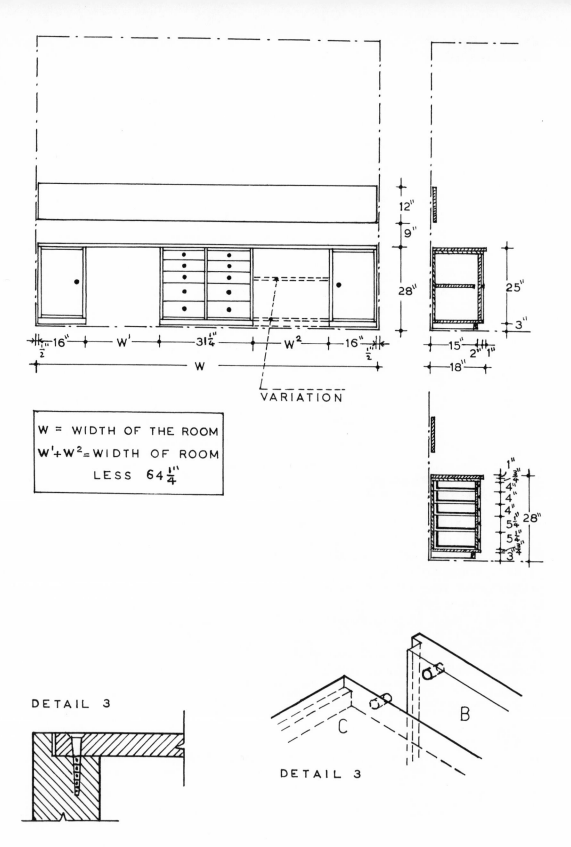

VARIATION

W = WIDTH OF THE ROOM
W' + W² = WIDTH OF ROOM
LESS 64¼"

12"
9"
28"

25"
3"

16" W' 31¼" W² 16"
½" ½"
W

15" 2" 1"
18"

1"
4"
4"
4"
5¼"
5¼"
3"
28"

DETAIL 3

C

B

DETAIL 3

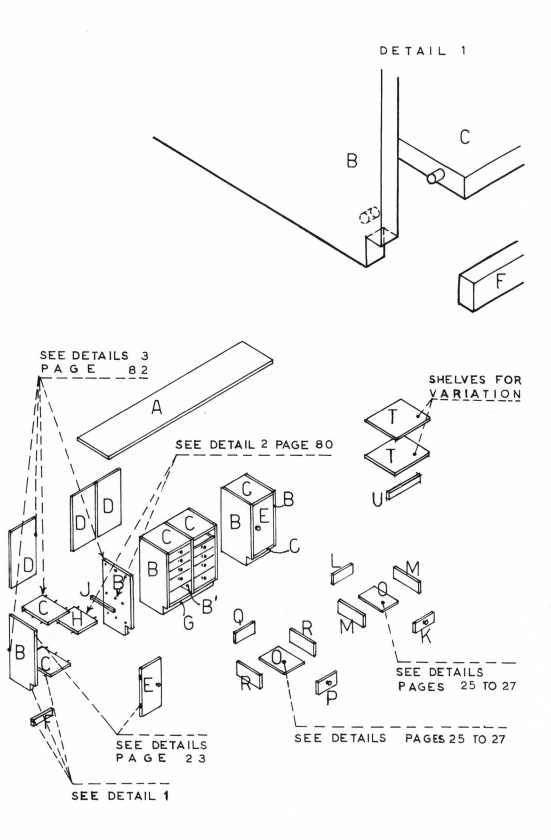

DETAIL 1

B

C

F

SEE DETAILS 3
PAGE 82

A

SEE DETAIL 2 PAGE 80

SHELVES FOR
VARIATION

T

T

U

D

D

D

D

G

B

B

E

C

C

C

C

B

B

J

B

H

G

B'

G

E

F

L

M

Q

Q

M

K

Q

R

M

R

O

R

P

SEE DETAILS
PAGES 25 TO 27

SEE DETAILS
PAGE 23

SEE DETAIL 1

SEE DETAILS PAGES 25 TO 27

4.3 TYPEWRITER DESK

Building this "portable typewriter" desk requires a little more skill and accuracy than the desk of Project 4.1, but your efforts will be amply rewarded. The top drawer front is made half height to permit free travel of the typewriter carriage. Commercial drawer slides may be substituted if desired.

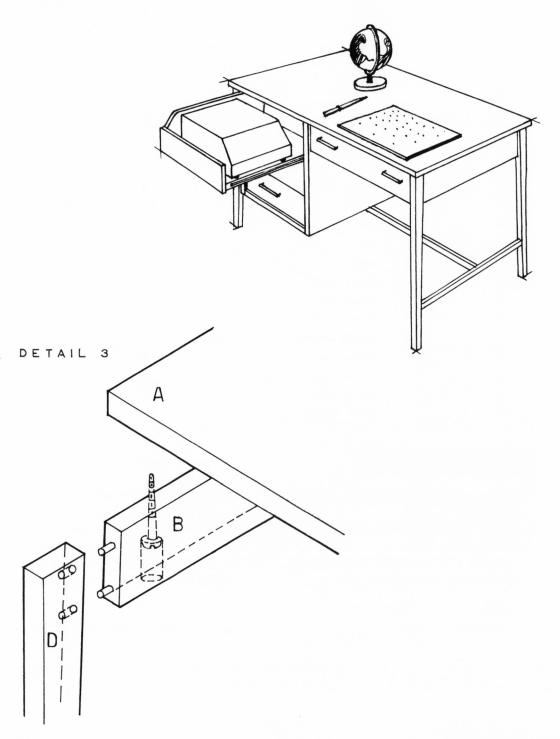

DETAIL 3

A

B

D

List of Materials

PART	NO.	FUNCTION	DIMENSION IN INCHES thickness	× width	× length
A	1	top	1	26	44
B	2	rails	¾	4½	20½
C	1	rail	¾	4	22
D	4	legs	1	2	28
E	2	stretchers	1	1¼	23
F	1	stretcher	1	1¼	42
G	2	sides	¾	23	20¾
H	1	back	¾	16½	20
J	1	bottom	¾	16½	23
K	2	pieces	¾	2	18
L	9	cleats	⅜	¾	21
M	1	drawer front	¾	4½	16½
O	1	bottom	¾	15	20½
P	1	side	¾	9	21¼
Q	1	back	¾	9	15¾
R	1	piece	¾	1¼	21¼
S	2	drawer fronts	¾	5½	16½
T	4	drawer sides	½	5½	21¾
U	2	drawer backs	½	5½	15½
V	2	drawer bottoms	¼	16	21½
W	1	drawer front	¾	4½	22
X	2	drawer sides	½	4½	21¾
Y	1	drawer back	½	4	21
Z	1	drawer bottom	¼	21	21½

Instructions for Assembly

1. Join rails (B) and stretchers (E) with legs (D).
2. Fasten sides (G) with back (H), bottom (J) and pieces (K).
3. Join rail (C), sides (G), stretcher (F) with legs (D) and stretcher (E).
4. Attach cleats (L) to sides (B) and (G) and fasten top to rails (B), (C) and (K) with screws.
5. Join drawer sides (P) and (R) with bottom (O), front (M) and back (Q).
6. Join drawer sides (T) with drawer fronts (S), backs (U) and install bottoms (V).
7. Join drawer sides (X) with drawer front (W) and back (Y) and install bottom (Z).
8. Apply finish.

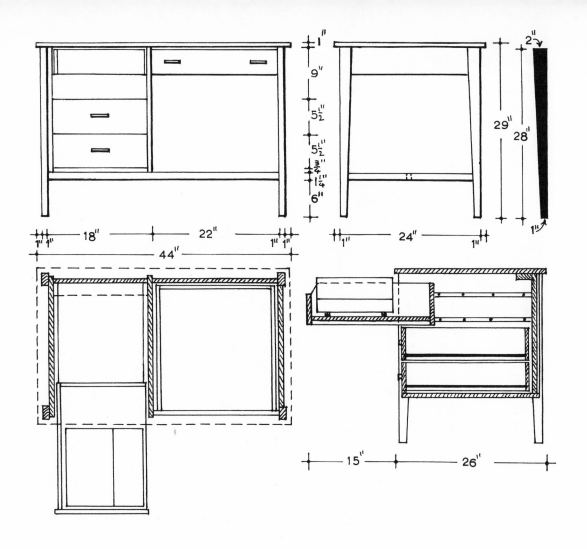

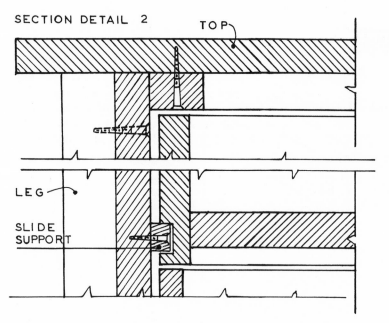

SECTION DETAIL 2

TOP

LEG

SLIDE
SUPPORT

Typewriter Desk

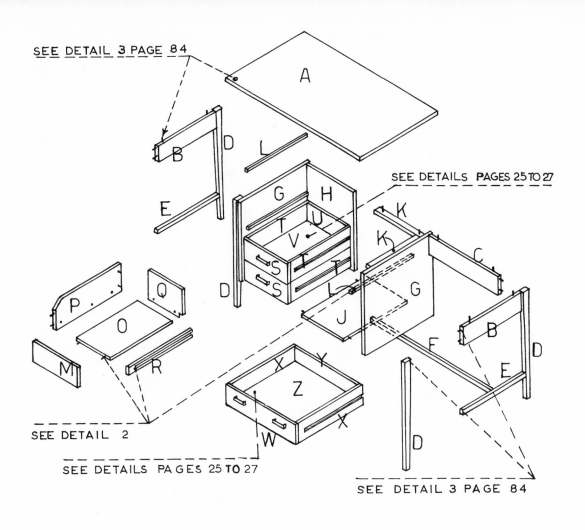

SEE DETAIL 3 PAGE 84

SEE DETAILS PAGES 25 TO 27

SEE DETAILS PAGES 25 TO 27

SEE DETAIL 2

SEE DETAIL 3 PAGE 84

DETAIL 2

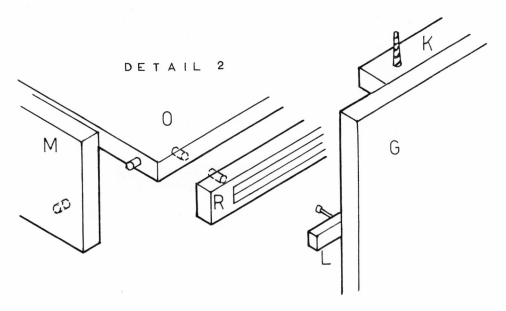

4.4 PLAY AND WORK TABLE

Made with sturdy legs for greater steadiness. Plywood top is covered with plastic material, and the raised edge keeps pencils and crayons off the floor.

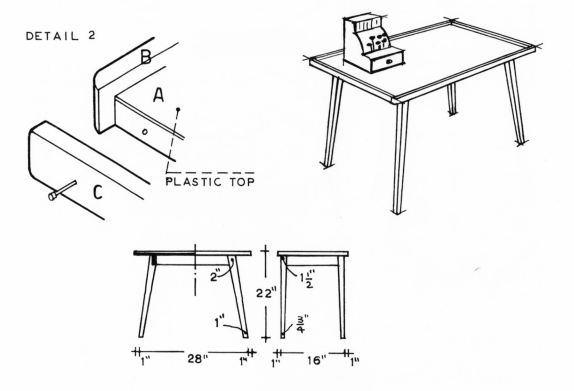

DETAIL 2

PLASTIC TOP

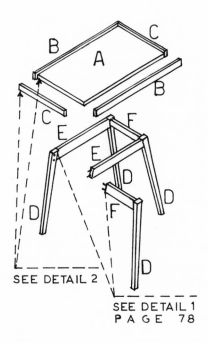

SEE DETAIL 2

SEE DETAIL 1
PAGE 78

List of Materials

PART	NO.	FUNCTION	DIMENSION IN INCHES		
			thickness × width × length		
A	1	top	$\frac{7}{8}$	17	29
B	2	strips	$\frac{1}{2}$	$1\frac{1}{8}$	30
C	2	strips	$\frac{1}{2}$	$1\frac{1}{8}$	17
D	4	legs	$1\frac{1}{2}$	2	$21\frac{1}{4}$
E	2	rails	$\frac{3}{4}$	2	18
F	2	rails	$\frac{3}{4}$	2	13

Instructions for Assembly

1. Attach strips (B) and (C) to top (A).
2. Join rails (E) to legs (D).
3. Fasten rails (F) to legs (D) and attach top (A) to rails (E) and (F) with screws.
4. Apply finish.

Play and Work Table

4.5 SMALL TABLE

Ideal for cozy tea parties (simulated) and board games of the younger set. Can be combined with the plywood chair of Project 4.9 to make an attractive two-piece unit. The corners are easily rounded—for added safety.

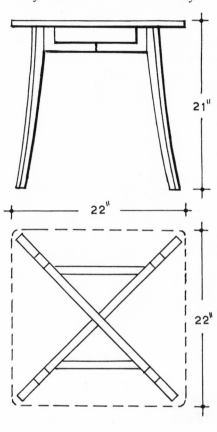

List of Materials

PART	NO.	FUNCTION	DIMENSION IN INCHES thickness × width × length		
A	1	top	¾	22	22
B	2	rails	1	2½	19
C	2	braces	1	1¾	12
D	4	legs	1	2½	21

Instructions for Assembly

1. Fasten rails (B) to legs (D).
2. Join rails (B) together.
3. Attach braces (C) to rails (B).
4. Fasten top (A) to rails (B).
5. Apply finish.

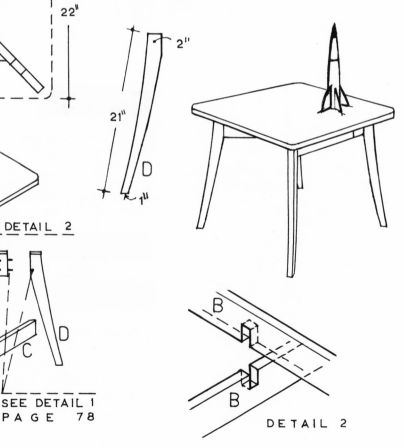

SEE DETAIL 2

SEE DETAIL 1
PAGE 78

DETAIL 2

4.6 STOOL

Tip-proof and sturdy, it can serve equally well as a seat, a stand for gadgets like radios and hamster cages, or occasionally as a night table. A good project to start on before working up to the more complicated items like desks.

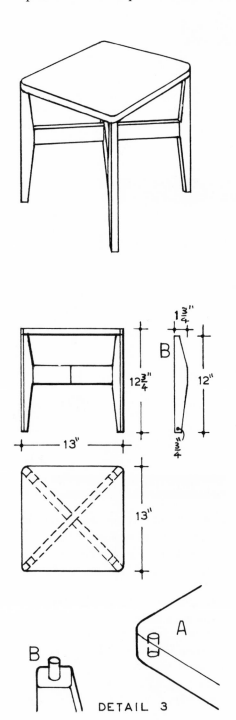

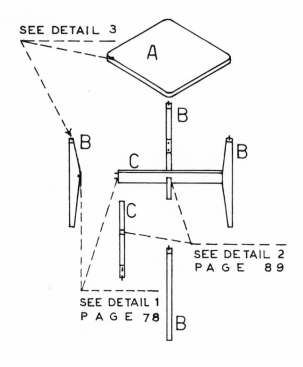

SEE DETAIL 3

A

B

B

C

B

B

SEE DETAIL 2
PAGE 89

SEE DETAIL 1
PAGE 78 B

List of Materials

PART	NO.	FUNCTION	DIMENSION IN INCHES thickness × width × length		
			thickness	width	length
A	1	top	¾	13	13
B	4	legs	1	1¾	12
C	2	rails	1	2	14

Instructions for Assembly

1. Attach legs (B) to rails (C).
2. Join rails (C).
3. Fasten top (A) to legs (B) with dowels.
4. Apply finish.

DETAIL 3

Stool

4.7 WORK TABLE

This is one of the most useful, all-purpose items for play, work and storage. The raised rim prevents small objects from falling off. Material used is plywood throughout, except for the cross-rail support, which is solid wood. A laminated plastic surface such as Formica is ideal for clay, finger paints, potted plants, aquariums, and even occasional between-meal snacks!

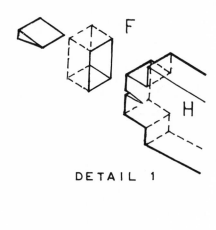

DETAIL 1

List of Materials

PART	NO.	FUNCTION	DIMENSION IN INCHES thickness × width × length		
A	1	top	½	14½	19
B	1	bottom	½	13½	19
C	2	sides	½	3½	14½
D	1	front	½	3½	20
E	1	back	½	2¾	19
F	1	support	¾	13	19½
G	1	support	¾	9	13½
H	1	rail	1¼	3	24
J	1	seat	¾	8	12
K	1	brace	1½	1½	11

Instructions for Assembly

1. Attach sides (C) to front (D) and back (E) and to bottom (B).
2. Install top (A) on front (D).
3. Join rails (H) to supports (F) and (G).
4. Fasten seat (J) to rails (H) and supports (G).
5. Join brace (K) to support (F) and fasten to bottom (B).
6. Apply finish.

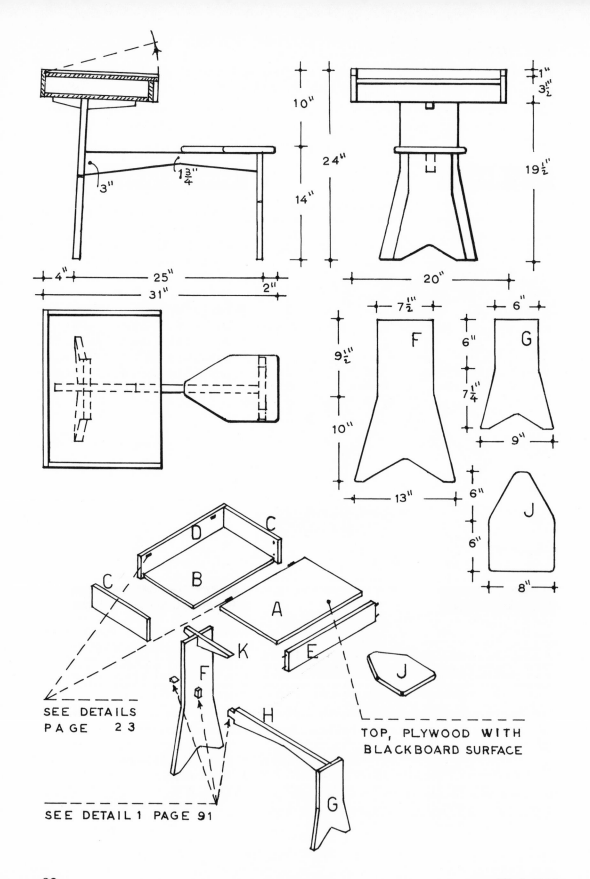

SEE DETAILS
PAGE 23

SEE DETAIL 1 PAGE 91

TOP, PLYWOOD WITH
BLACKBOARD SURFACE

Work Table

4.8 STANDARD CHAIR

Why build a "standard" chair when they can be bought so easily? Answer: it's more fun. Then, too, you can "tailor" it to match the other furniture in your child's room. Besides, think of the heirloom value!

List of Materials

PART	NO.	FUNCTION	DIMENSION IN INCHES thickness × width × length		
A	2	legs	1	3	31
B	2	legs	1	1¾	16¾
C	2	rails	¾	1¾	13½
D	2	rails	¾	1¾	13
E	1	rail	¾	1¼	13
F	1	seat	¾	17	18
G	1	back	½	6	16
H	2	stretchers	⅝ diam.		14
J	2	stretchers	⅝ diam.		16
K	4	corner blocks	1	2	2

Instructions for Assembly

1. Attach legs (A) and (B) to rails (C) and stretcher (J).
2. Join legs (A) and (B) to rails (E) and (D) and to stretchers (H).
3. Fasten corner blocks (K) and attach seat (F) with screws.
4. Fasten back (G) to rail (E) and legs (A) with screws.
5. Apply finish. *Note:* Seat can be upholstered with half-inch foam rubber, covered with either fabric or plastic.

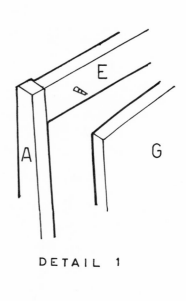

DETAIL 1

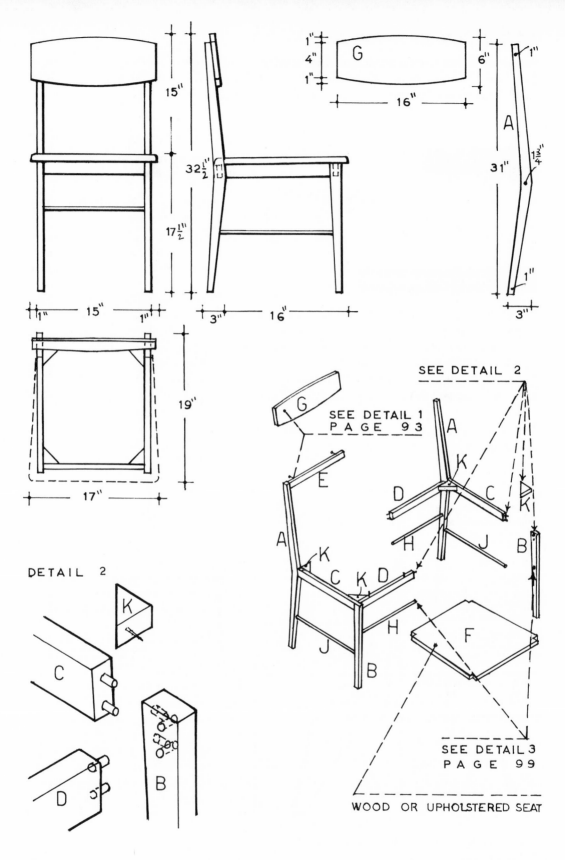

15"

32$\frac{1}{2}$"

17$\frac{1}{2}$"

1" 15" 1"

3" 16"

1"
4"
1"

16"

6"

A

31"

1$\frac{3}{4}$"

1"

3"

G

19"

17"

SEE DETAIL 2

G

SEE DETAIL 1
PAGE 93

E

A

A

D

K

C

H

J

K

B

K

C

K D

H

J

B

F

SEE DETAIL 3
PAGE 99

DETAIL 2

K

C

D

B

WOOD OR UPHOLSTERED SEAT

Standard Chair

4.9 PLYWOOD CHAIR

Simple in construction and designed for hard use, this practical chair has the shortest list of materials in the book. Makes an attractive companionpiece to the table of Project 4.5.

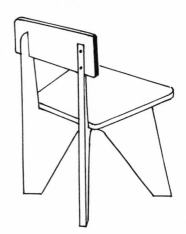

List of Materials

PART	NO.	FUNCTION	DIMENSION IN INCHES thickness × width × length		
A	1	plywood panel (finished both sides)	½	30	30

Instructions for Assembly

1. Enlarge drawing of parts to full scale and trace on plywood as indicated. Do not buy plywood with "rough finish" (knots in veneer) on one side; both sides must be "smooth finish."
2. Join together cross supports (C) and (D).
3. Attach seat (A) to cross supports (C) and (D) with screws.
4. Fasten back (B) to cross supports (C) and (D).
5. Apply finish.

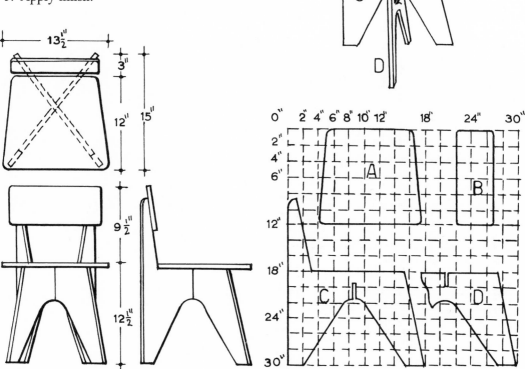

SEE DETAIL 2 PAGE 89

4.10 STEP STOOL

Secondary but eminently useful—for climbing, reaching, sitting, and as a footrest in the bathroom. Easy and inexpensive to make.

List of Materials

SEE DETAIL 1 PAGE 115

PART	NO.	FUNCTION	DIMENSION IN INCHES thickness × width × length		
			thickness	width	length
A	1	step	¾	9	15
B	1	step	¾	6¾	15
C	2	sides	¾	12	15¾
D	2	rails	1	2	12

Instructions for Assembly

1. Join sides (C) with rails (D).
2. Fasten steps (A) and (B) to sides (C) and rails (D).
3. Apply finish.

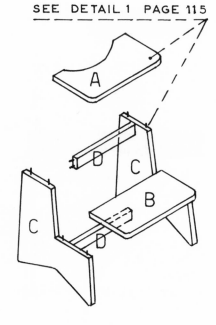

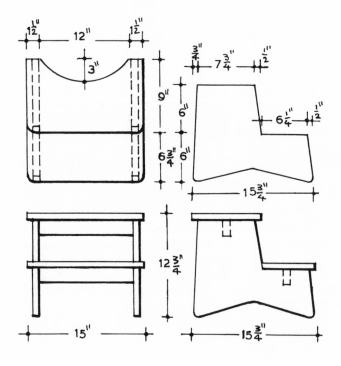

4.11 ROCKING CHAIR

Children love to "cruise" in a rocking chair, and it's good exercise. This simple design with solid wood frame and plywood seat and back is just right size, too.

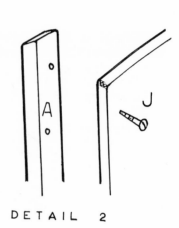

DETAIL 2

List of Materials

PART	NO.	FUNCTION	DIMENSION IN INCHES		
			thickness ×	width ×	length
A	2	legs	1	1½	22
B	2	legs	1	1½	15
C	2	arms	1	1½	17½
D	2	bases	2½	1½	25
E	1	rail	½	1½	14
F	2	rails	¾	1½	14
G	2	rails	¾	1½	16
H	1	seat	½	17	18
J	1	back	½	6	17½

Instructions for Assembly

1. Attach arms (C), rails (G) and bases (D) to legs (A) and (B).
2. Join rails (E) and (F) to legs (A) and (B) and to base (D).
3. Attach seat (H) to rails (F) and (G) with screws.
4. Fasten back (J) to legs (A).
5. Apply finish.

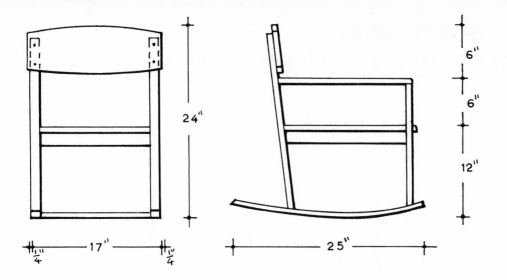

24"

6"

6"

12"

17"

¼"

¼"

25"

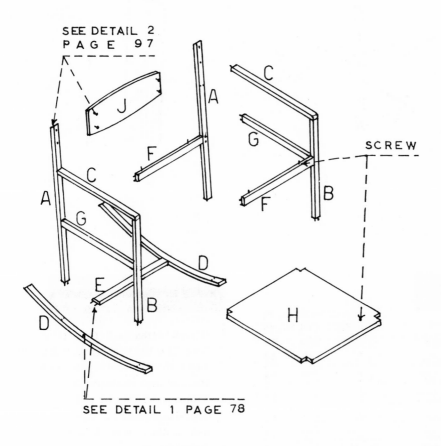

SEE DETAIL 2
PAGE 97

J

A

C

F

G

SCREW

C

A

G

B

F

D

E

B

D

H

SEE DETAIL 1 PAGE 78

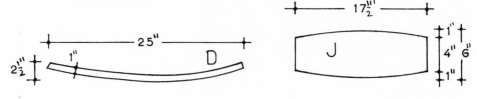

25"

1"

2½"

D

17½"

1"

4" 6"

1"

J

Rocking Chair

4.12 JUNIOR CHAIR OR HIGH STOOL

More grown-up and dignified than the high chair of Project 1.4, this easy-to-make item allows junior to eat right off the dining-room table. The foot rest is strictly for comfort.

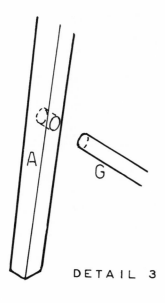

DETAIL 3

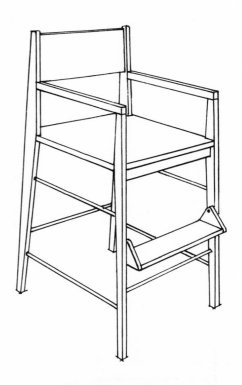

List of Materials

PART	NO.	FUNCTION	DIMENSION IN INCHES thickness × width × length		
A	2	legs	1	2½	36
B	2	legs	1	1¾	27¾
C	2	arms	1	1¼	15
D	1	back	½	7	14
E	1	seat	¾	16	16
F	2	rails	¾	1¾	14
G	4	stretchers	⅝ diam.		17
H	2	stretchers	⅝		15
J	2	supports	½	4	5
K	1	support	½	5	13

Instructions for Assembly

1. Attach legs (A) and (B) to arms (C) and stretchers (G).
2. Join legs (A) and (B) to back (D) and rails (F) and stretchers (H).
3. Fasten seat (E) to rails (F) with screws.
4. Join supports (J) and (K) together and fasten to legs (B) with screws.
5. Apply finish.

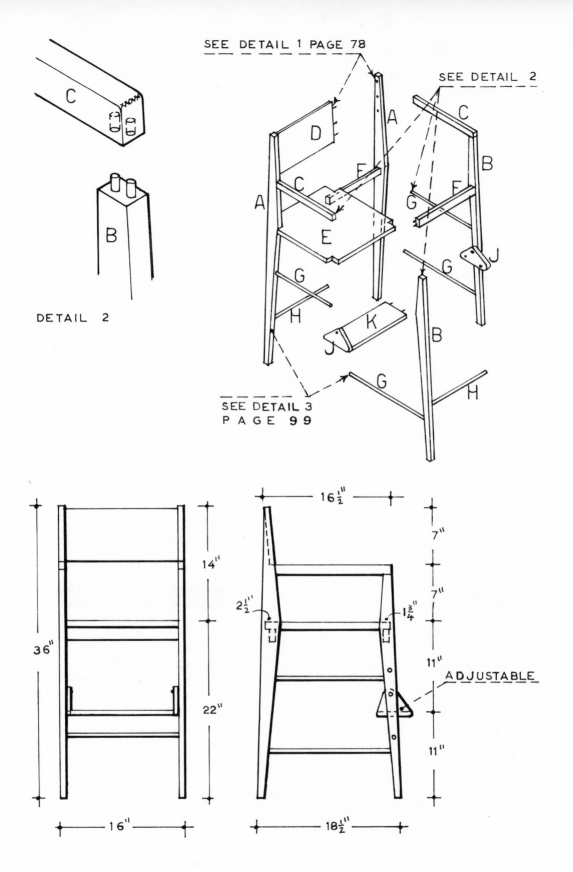

SEE DETAIL 1 PAGE 78

SEE DETAIL 2

DETAIL 2

SEE DETAIL 3
PAGE 99

16 1/2"

7"

7"

2 1/2"

1 3/4"

11"

ADJUSTABLE

11"

14"

22"

36"

16"

18 1/2"

4.13 WORKBENCH

The smart way to save Dad's tools is to give Junior his own—and a workbench scaled to his own size and needs. When he sees you building this he'll want to try one of these projects himself. The top is made of solid boards glued together.

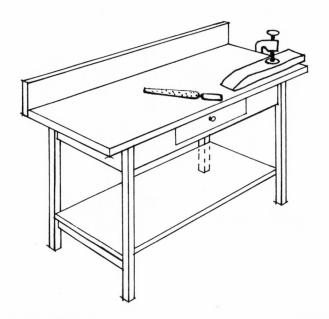

List of Materials

PART	NO.	FUNCTION	DIMENSION IN INCHES thickness × width × length		
			thickness	width	length
A	1	top	1¼	18	42
B	1	back	1	5¼	42
C	4	legs	2	2	28¾
D	1	bottom	¾	15	36
E	2	framing pieces	1	5	32
F	2	side pieces	1	5	13
G	2	side rails	1	1½	13
H	2	drawer slides	1¼	1¼	14
J	1	drawer fronts	¾	3½	18
K	2	drawer sides	½	3½	13¾
L	1	drawer back	½	3	17
M	1	drawer bottom	¼	13½	17½
O	4	corner blocks	1	3	3

Instructions for Assembly

1. Join legs (C) to sides (F) and (G).
2. Fasten framing pieces (E) to legs (C) and attach corner blocks (O).
3. Join back (B) with top (A).
4. Fasten drawer slide (H) to side (E).
5. Assemble drawer by joining side (K) with front (J) and back (L) and attaching bottom (M).
6. Apply finish.

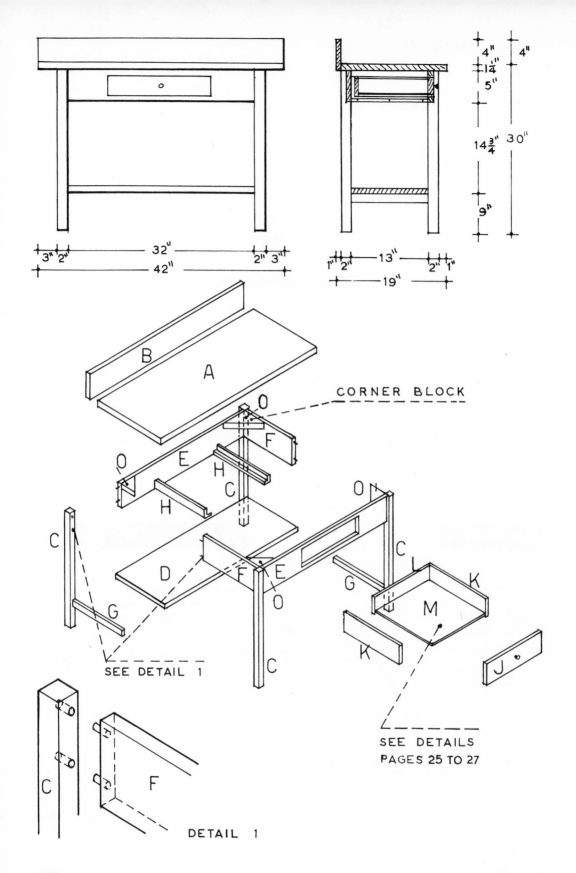

CORNER BLOCK

SEE DETAIL 1

SEE DETAILS
PAGES 25 TO 27

DETAIL 1

SECTION 5: STORAGE UNITS

5.1 WARDROBE

Here's a piece of furniture that grows with the child! Both shelves and clothespole may be raised as the little man (or lady) gets taller. Standing a full six feet from the floor, the wardrobe can even be used by adults if one shelf is removed.

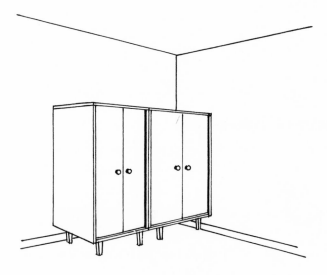

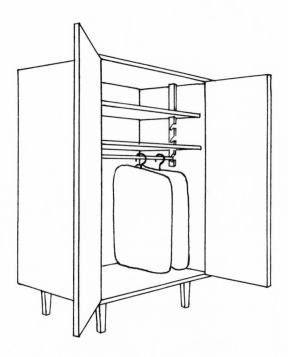

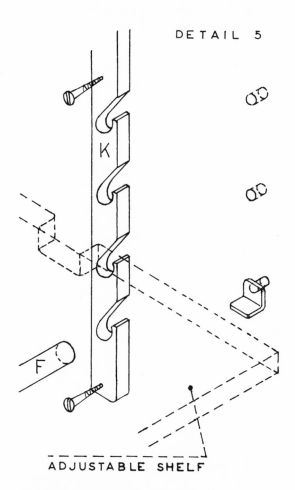

DETAIL 5

K

F

ADJUSTABLE SHELF

1. Join top and bottom (A) with sides (B).
2. Install back (C).
3. Fasten strips (K).
4. Join rails (H) and (J) to legs (G) and attach base to bottom (A) with screws.
5. Attach doors (D) to sides (B) and install pipe (F) and shelf (E).
6. Apply finish.

List of Materials

PART	NO.	FUNCTION	DIMENSION IN INCHES		
			thickness ×	width ×	length
A	2	pieces	¾	24	34½
B	2	sides	¾	24	64
C	1	back	¼	35½	63½
D	2	doors	¾	17¼	62½
E	2	shelves	¾	22	34½
F	1	pipe	1 diam.		34½
G	4	legs	1	1¾	8
H	2	rails	1	1¾	19
J	1	rail	1	1¾	25½
K	2	strips	½	2	30

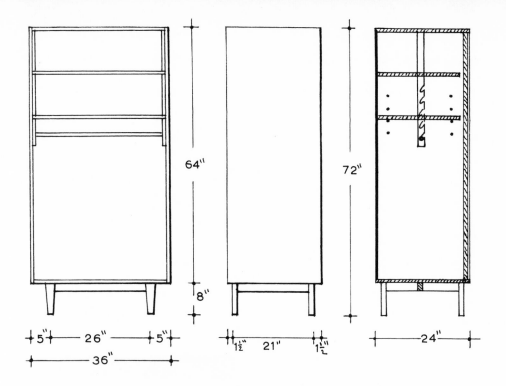

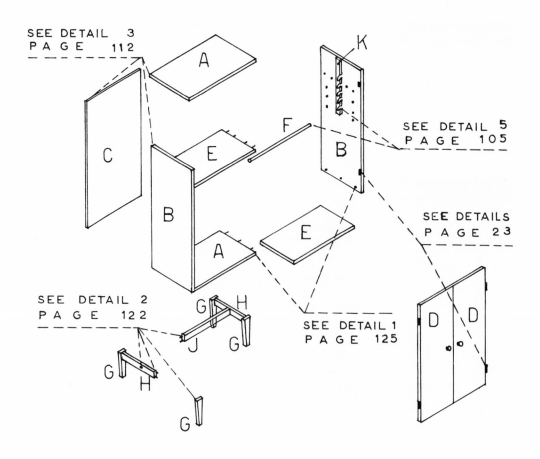

SEE DETAIL 3
PAGE 112

SEE DETAIL 5
PAGE 105

SEE DETAILS
PAGE 23

SEE DETAIL 2
PAGE 122

SEE DETAIL 1
PAGE 125

Wardrobe

5.2 LOW CHEST

Made of plywood with solid wood base, this is attractive and serviceable—and will stand a lot of rough usage from busy teen-agers, which might not be true of an expensive store-bought piece. The addition of a wall mirror converts it into a dresser.

List of Materials

PART	NO.	FUNCTION	DIMENSION IN INCHES		
			thickness ×	width ×	length
A	1	top	¾	17	36
B	1	bottom	¾	17	34½
C	2	sides	¾	17	21¼
D	1	back	¼	21½	35½
E	1	partition	¾	9½	16¾
F	2	rails	¾	2	16⅞
G	2	rails	¾	2	34½
H	10	cleats	¾	1	14¾
J	4	drawer fronts	¾	4	16⅞
K	8	drawer sides	½	4	16⅜
L	4	drawer backs	½	3½	15⅞
M	4	drawer bottoms	¼	16⅜	16¼
N	4	drawer sides	½	5⅛	16⅜
O	2	drawer fronts	¾	5⅛	34½
P	2	drawer backs	½	4⅝	33½
Q	2	drawer bottoms	¼	34	16¼
R	4	legs	1½	1½	8
S	2	rails	¾	1½	27
T	2	rails	¾	1½	12½

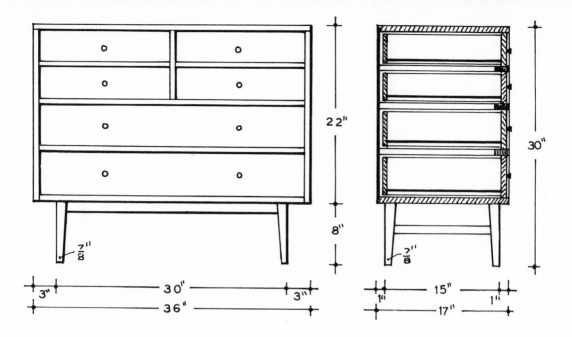

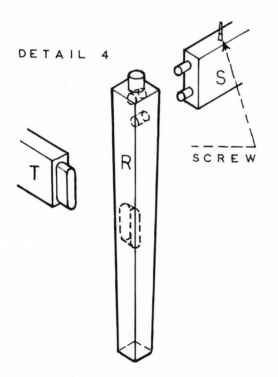

DETAIL 4

SCREW

Instructions for Assembly

1. Join bottom (B), partition (E), rails (F, G) to side (C).
2. Attach top (A) and back (D).
3. Fasten cleats (H) to side (C) and partition (E).
4. Join drawer sides (K) to drawer fronts (J) and backs (L), and install bottoms (M).
5. Join drawer sides (N) to drawer fronts (O) and backs (P), and install bottoms (Q).
6. Fasten rails (S) and (T) to legs (R).
7. Attach rails (S) to bottom (C) with screws.
8. Apply finish.

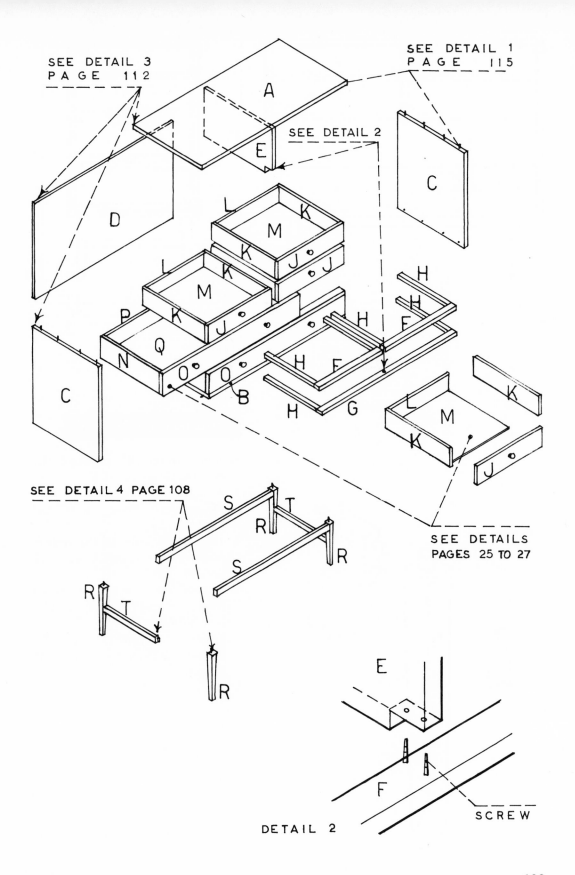

SEE DETAIL 3
PAGE 112

SEE DETAIL 1
PAGE 115

A

SEE DETAIL 2

E

C

L
K
M
K
J
J

L
K
M
K
J

D

C

P
Q
N
O
O
B

H
H
H
F
H
F
H
F
H
G

L
K
M
K
J
K
J

SEE DETAIL 4 PAGE 108

S
T
R
R
S
R

R
T
R

SEE DETAILS
PAGES 25 TO 27

E

F

SCREW

DETAIL 2

5.3 HIGH CHEST

As every homeowner knows, factory-built chests like these are expensive items, and their fine wood finishes soon develop nicks and scratches. This homemade version will serve the purpose just as well—and save you many dollars. Like the low chest of Project 5.2, this is also of plywood, with solid wood base.

PART	NO.	FUNCTION	DIMENSION IN INCHES		
			thickness ×	width ×	length
A	1	top	¾	17	32
B	2	sides	¾	17	33¾
C	1	bottom	¾	17	30½
D	1	back	¼	31½	34
E	4	rails	¾	2	30½
F	8	cleats	¾	1	14¾
G	5	drawer fronts	¾	6	30½
H	5	drawer backs	½	5½	29½
J	10	drawer sides	½	6	16⅜
K	5	drawer bottoms	¼	16¼	30
L	4	legs	1½	1½	8
M	2	rails	¾	1½	24
O	2	rails	¾	1½	12½

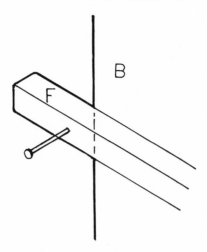

Instructions for Assembly

1. Join bottom (C) and rails (E) with side (B).
2. Install top (A) and back (D).
3. Attach cleats (F).
4. Join drawer sides (J) with drawer fronts (G) and backs (H) and install bottoms (K).
5. Fasten legs (L) to rails (M) and (O) and attach rails (M) to bottom (C) with screws.
6. Apply finish.

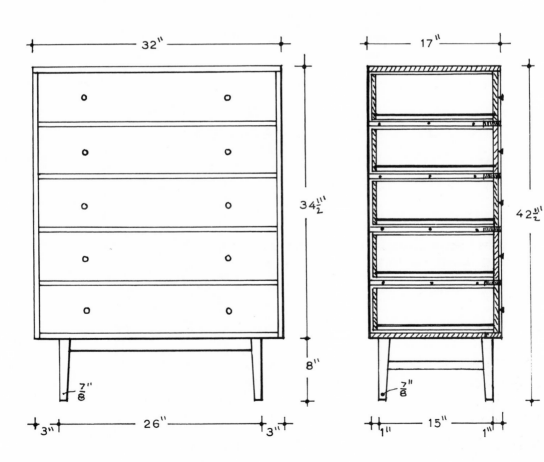

High Chest

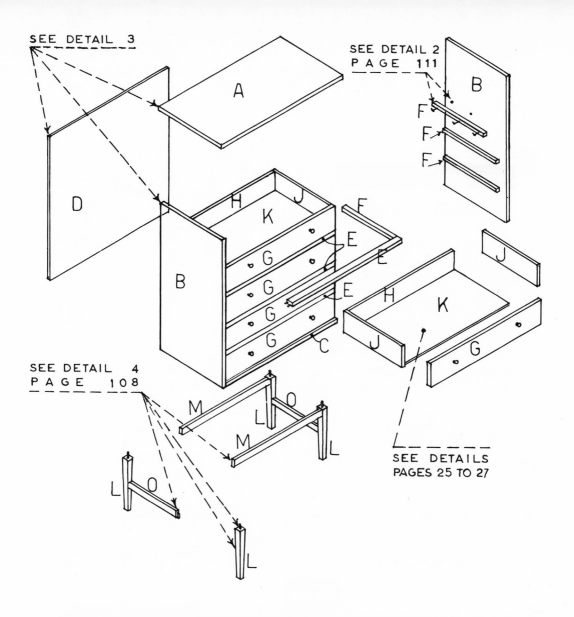

SEE DETAIL 3

A

SEE DETAIL 2
PAGE 111

B

F
F
F

D

H J
K
B
E
E
G E
G
G
C
G

F
J

H
K
J
G

SEE DETAIL 4
PAGE 108

M O
L
M
L
L O
L

SEE DETAILS
PAGES 25 TO 27

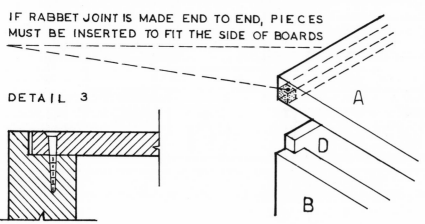

IF RABBET JOINT IS MADE END TO END, PIECES
MUST BE INSERTED TO FIT THE SIDE OF BOARDS

DETAIL 3

A

D

B

High Chest

5.4 STORAGE CABINET

No child ever has enough space for storing things, but this cabinet will be a step in the right direction. Designed to serve from toddlerhood to adulthood. Best of all, it's easy to put together.

PART	NO.	FUNCTION	thickness	×	width	×	length
A	1	top	¾		15		W
B	1	shelf	¾		14¾		× W less 1½
C	1	bottom	¾		15		× W less 1½
D	2	sides	¾		15		32¼
E	1	back	¼		32½		× W less ½
F	6	partitions	¾		14¾		15⅜
G	2	doors	¾		15⅜		16½
H	1	toeplate	¾		3		W
J	2	toeplates	¾		3		12
K	2	corner blocks	¾		3		3

DIMENSION IN INCHES

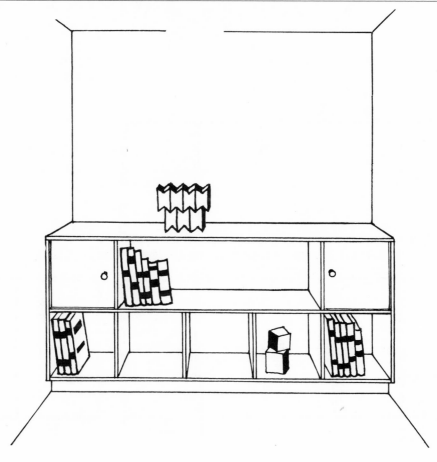

Instructions for Assembly

1. Fasten shelf (B) and bottom (C) to partitions (F) and sides (D).
2. Attach top (A) and install back (E).
3. Join toeplates (H) and (J) to corner blocks (K) and fasten to bottom (C).
4. Install doors (G) on side (D).
5. Apply finish and set cabinet in place.

W = WIDTH OF THE ROOM

W' = WIDTH OF THE ROOM
LESS 37"

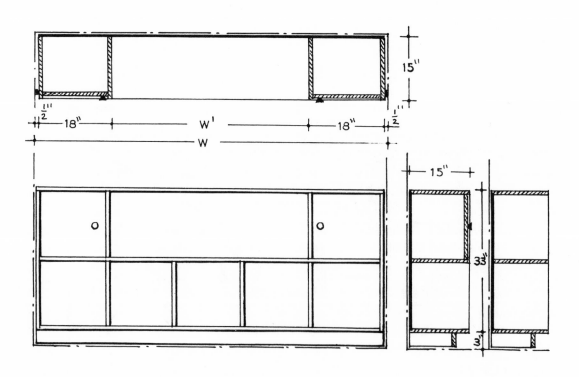

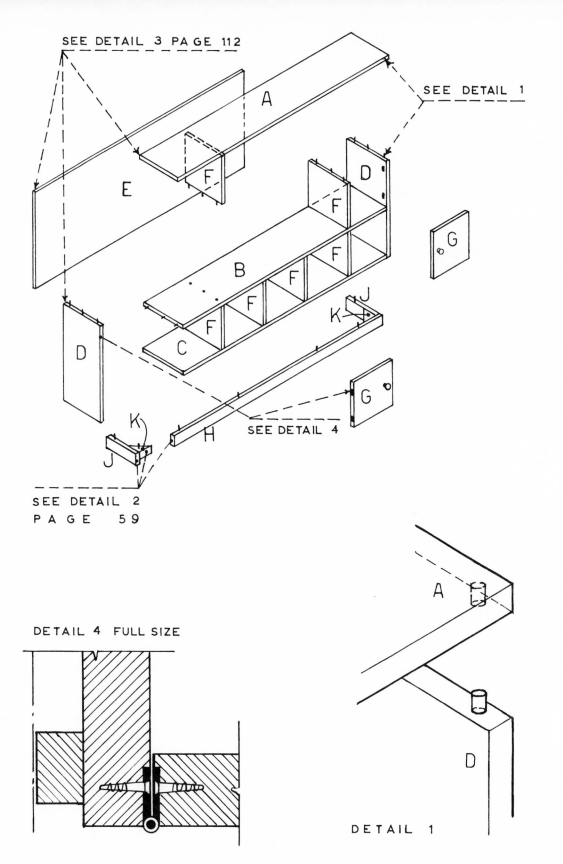

SEE DETAIL 3 PAGE 112

A

SEE DETAIL 1

E

F

D

F

F

F

B

F

G

F

F

J

K

D

C

K

H

SEE DETAIL 4

G

J

SEE DETAIL 2
PAGE 59

DETAIL 4 FULL SIZE

A

D

DETAIL 1

Storage Cabinet

5.5 TOY CHEST AND BENCH

The addition of the graceful back and sides takes this practical storage bin out of the foot-locker category; its very appearance encourages neatness. A word of advice: don't use it to store broken, discarded toys and "junk," so that it loses half its utility.

List of Materials

PART	NO.	FUNCTION	DIMENSION IN INCHES thickness × width × length		
A	2	sides	¾	15½	16
B	2	panels	¾	7½	28½
C	1	bottom	¾	13½	28½
D	1	top	¾	13½	28½
E	1	board	¾	2	28½
F	1	back	¾	3	28½
G	8	dowels	⅜ diam.		7
H	4	legs	1¼ top diam.		4

Instructions for Assembly

1. Join panels (B) to bottom (C).
2. Insert dowels (G) in rails (E, F).
3. Fasten side (A) to (B), (C), (E) and (F).
4. Install top (D) on board (E) with two hinges.
5. Attach legs (H) to bottom (C).
6. Apply finish.

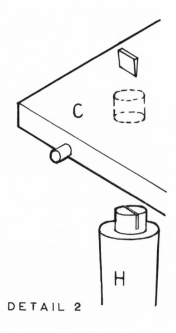

DETAIL 2

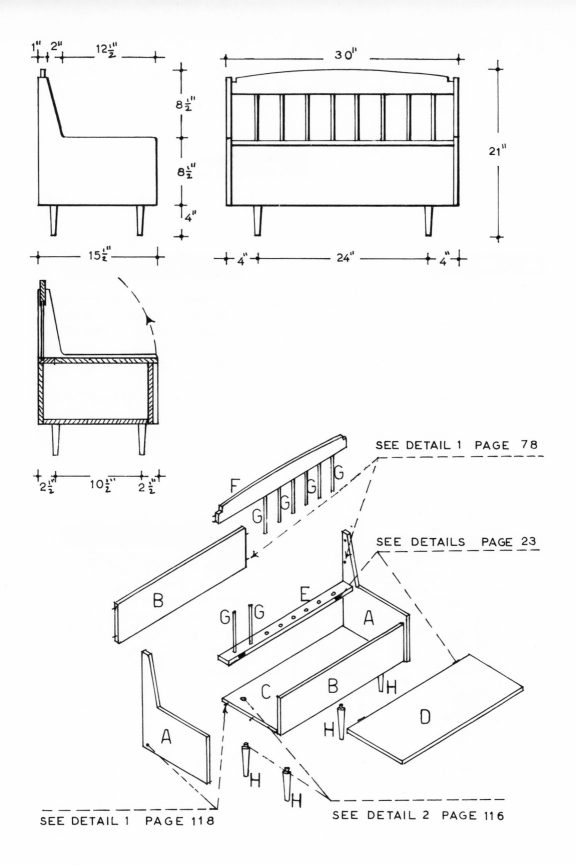

1" 2" 12½" 8½" 8½" 4" 15½" 2½" 10½" 2½"

30" 21" 4" 24" 4"

SEE DETAIL 1 PAGE 78

F G G G G G

SEE DETAILS PAGE 23

B

E A

G G

C B H

A D

H H H

SEE DETAIL 1 PAGE 118

SEE DETAIL 2 PAGE 116

5.6 TAPERED BOOKSHELVES

The tapering not only enlivens the appearance of this simple piece but also provides deep storage space on the lower shelf. Frame and shelves are of plywood, with legs of solid wood.

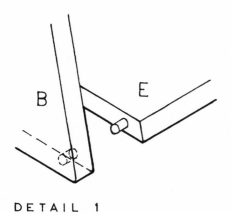

DETAIL 1

List of Materials

PART	NO.	FUNCTION	DIMENSION IN INCHES thickness × width × length		
A	1	back	½	41½	40
B	2	sides	¾	15	41
C	1	shelf	¾	10	40½
D	1	shelf	¾	12½	40½
E	1	bottom	¾	15	42
F	4	legs	1½	1½	7
G	1	rail	1	1½	29
H	2	rails	1	1½	9

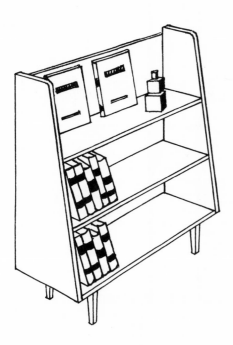

Instructions for Assembly

1. Join shelves (C) and (D) and bottom (E) to sides (B).
2. Install back (A).
3. Fasten rails (H) to legs (F).
4. Join rail (G) to rails (H) and attach legs to bottom (E).
5. Apply finish.

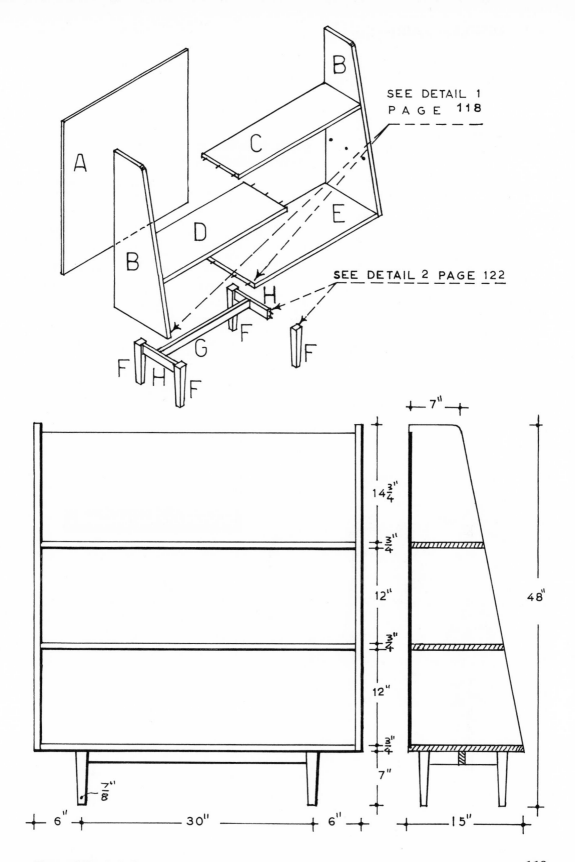

SEE DETAIL 1
PAGE 118

SEE DETAIL 2 PAGE 122

Tapered Bookshelves

5.7 DISPLAY CABINET

This professional-looking piece lends an air of neatness to a room and protects fragile models, sculpture, trophies and souvenirs from dust and damage. The shallow drawers behind doors are ideal for collections of rocks, shells, microscope slides, butterflies, leaves and the like.

List of Materials

PART	NO.	FUNCTION	thickness	×	width	×	length
A	1	top	¾		15		54
B	2	shelves	¾		14¾		52½
C	1	bottom	¾		15		52½
D	2	sides	¾		15		45¼
E	1	back	¼		45½		53½
F	2	partitions	¾		14¾		17
G	4	plate glass doors	¼		13½		26¾
H	3	doors	¾		17		17
J	4	tray fronts	¾		4¼		16
K	4	backs	½		3¾		15
L	8	sides	½		4¼		13¼
M	4	bottoms	¼		15½		13
O	4	legs	1½		1½		7
P	2	rails	1		1¾		10¼
Q	1	rail	1		1¾		41¼
R	8	cleats	⅜		¾		12½
S	1	filler	1		13½		17

DIMENSION IN INCHES

Instructions for Assembly

1. Join top (A), shelves (B), partition (F) and bottom (C) to sides (D).
2. Install back (E).
3. Attach filler (S) to side (D) and fasten cleats (R) to partition (F) and filler (S).
4. Join tray sides (L) to fronts and backs (J, K) and install bottom (M).
5. Fasten rails (P) to legs (O).
6. Join rail (Q) to rails (P) and attach base to bottom (C).
7. Attach door (H) to side (D) and partition (F).
8. Apply finish.
9. Install plate glass doors (G).

SPACE FOR
REMOVAL
OF DOOR

DETAIL 4
FULL SIZE

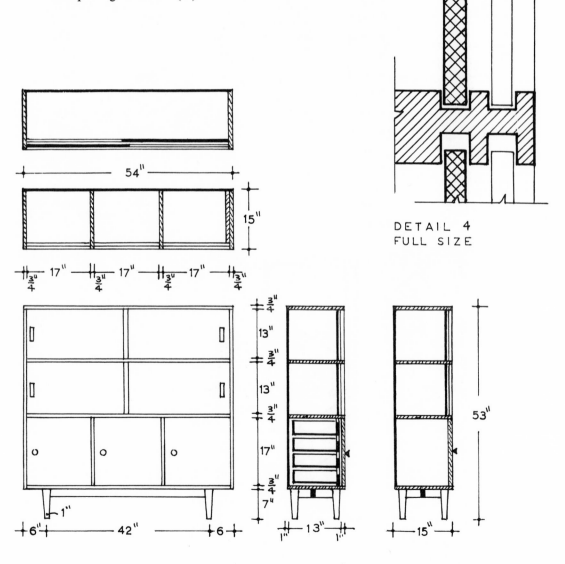

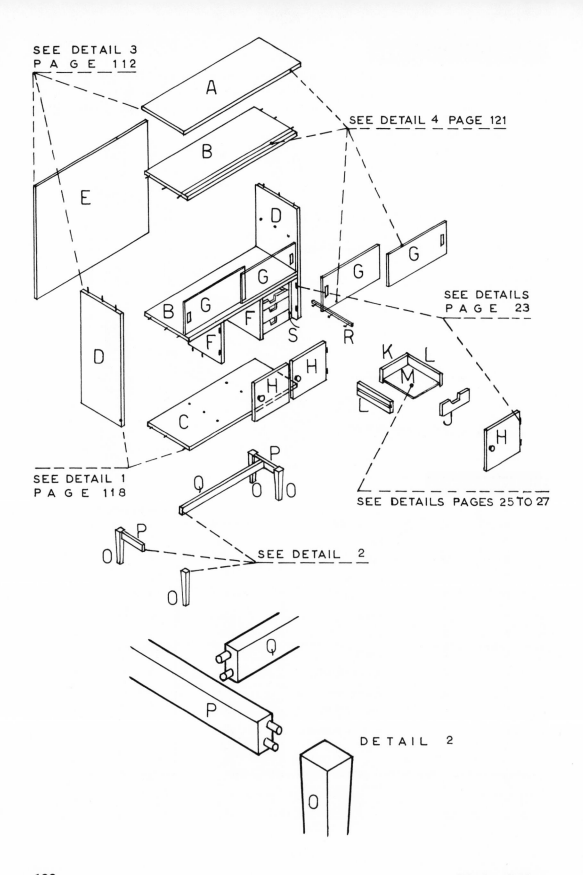

SEE DETAIL 3
P A G E 112

SEE DETAIL 4 PAGE 121

SEE DETAILS
P A G E 23

SEE DETAILS PAGES 25 TO 27

SEE DETAIL 1
P A G E 118

SEE DETAIL 2

DETAIL 2

5.8 CHIFFOROBE

Like the wardrobe of Project 5.1, this practical piece "grows" with the user; when the dress compartment becomes too small it can be used as a cabinet by adding shelves. The chiffo-robe matches the chests of Projects 5.2 and 5.3, making a bedroom set of two or three pieces.

List of Materials

PART	NO.	FUNCTION	DIMENSION IN INCHES		
			thickness	× width ×	length
A	1	top	¾	17	45
B	2	sides	¾	17	27
C	1	partition	¾	16¾	26¼
D	1	bottom	¾	17	43½
E	1	back	¼	27¼	44½
F	3	rails	¾	2	25
G	6	cleats	¾	1	14¾
H	4	drawer fronts	¾	6	25
J	4	drawer backs	¾	5½	24
K	8	drawer sides	½	6	16⅜
L	4	drawer bottoms	¼	16¼	24½
M	4	legs	1½	1½	8
O	2	rails	¾	1½	34
P	2	rails	¾	1½	14½
Q	1	door	¾	26¼	17¾
R	1	dowel or pipe	1 diam.		17¾

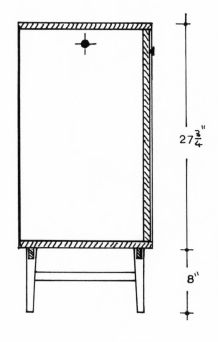

$27\frac{3}{4}$"

8"

Instructions for Assembly

1. Join bottom (D), partition (C), rails (F) to sides (B).
2. Attach top (A) and back (E).
3. Fasten cleats (G) and pipe (R) to sides (B) and partition (C).
4. Join drawer sides (K) to fronts (H) and backs (J) and install bottoms (L).
5. Fasten legs (M) to rails (O) and (P) and attach base to bottom (C) with screws.
6. Apply finish.

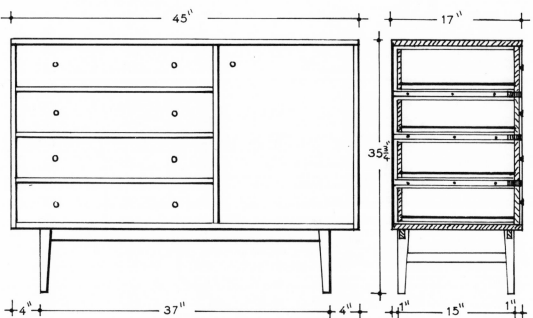

45"   17"

$35\frac{3}{4}$"

4"   37"   4"   1"   15"   1"

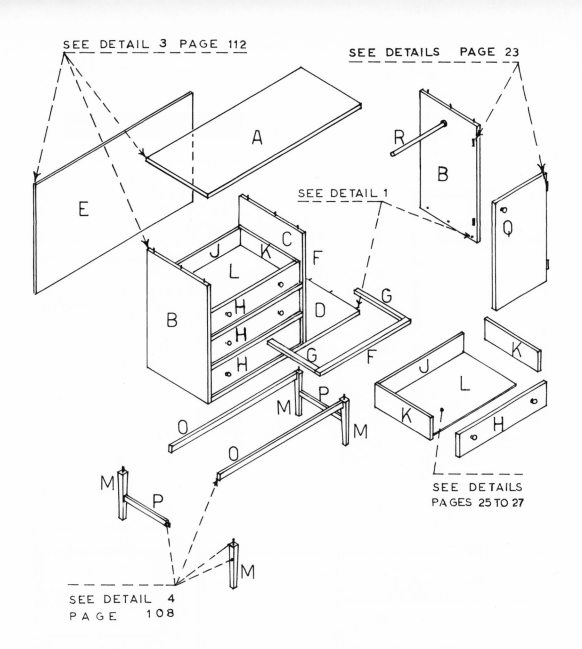

SEE DETAIL 3 PAGE 112

SEE DETAILS PAGE 23

A

E

R

B

SEE DETAIL 1

Q

J K C

F

L

B

H

D

G

H

G F

H

J

L

K

M P

O

M

K

H

O

M

P

M

SEE DETAILS
PAGES 25 TO 27

SEE DETAIL 4
PAGE 108

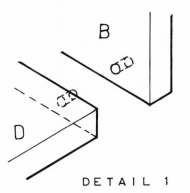

B

D

DETAIL 1

5.9 CHEST for stationery or art materials

We all know how a pad of expensive drawing or tracing paper can get dog-eared and shredded just "lying around." Here is a businesslike cabinet for storing all sorts and sizes of stationery, construction paper, crepe paper, water-color paper, pastel pencils, oil tubes, rulers and triangles. Plywood frame, with drawers of either plywood or solid wood. Drawer plates help keep things orderly.

PART	NO.	FUNCTION	DIMENSION IN INCHES		
			thickness ×	width ×	length
A	1	top	¾	18	24
B	2	sides	¾	24	27¼
C	1	bottom	¾	16½	24
D	1	back	¼	17½	25
E	1	toeplate	¾	2½	16½
F	12	cleats	⅜	¾	22½
G	6	drawer fronts	¾	4	16½
H	6	drawer backs	½	3½	15½
J	12	drawer sides	½	4	23¼
K	6	drawer bottoms	¼	16	23

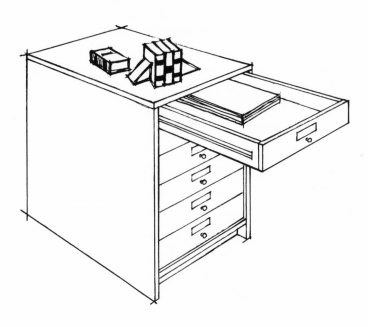

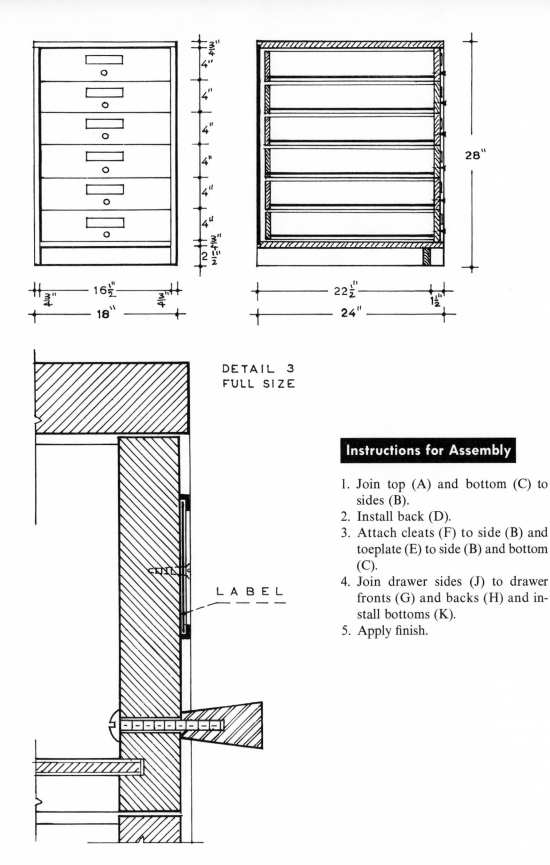

DETAIL 3
FULL SIZE

LABEL

Instructions for Assembly

1. Join top (A) and bottom (C) to sides (B).
2. Install back (D).
3. Attach cleats (F) to side (B) and toeplate (E) to side (B) and bottom (C).
4. Join drawer sides (J) to drawer fronts (G) and backs (H) and install bottoms (K).
5. Apply finish.

Chest for Stationery or Art Materials

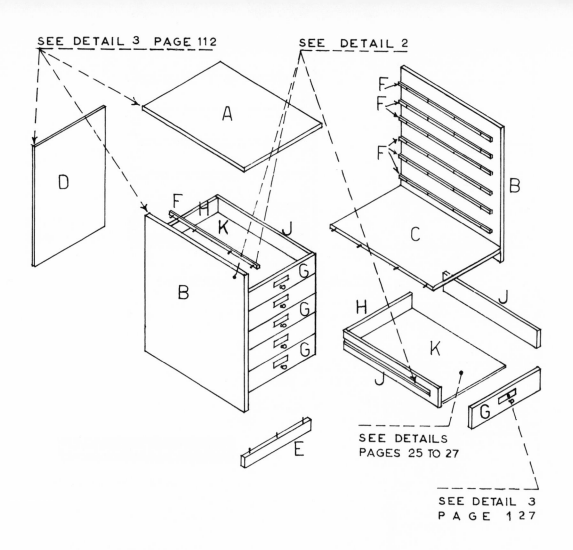

SEE DETAIL 3 PAGE 112

SEE DETAIL 2

A

D

F

F

F

B

B

F H

K

J

C

G

G

G

H

K

J

J

E

SEE DETAILS
PAGES 25 TO 27

G

SEE DETAIL 3
PAGE 127

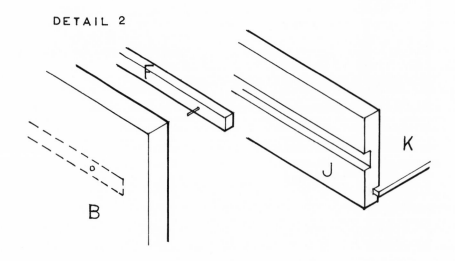

DETAIL 2

F

K

J

B

Chest for Stationery or Art Materials

SECTION 6: INDOOR PLAY EQUIPMENT

6.1 DOLL'S CRADLE

This is for a big doll, and is sturdy enough for a three-year-old's occasional nap. There's not much point in building a small cradle that won't take dolls from 14 to 22 inches long.

List of Materials

			DIMENSION IN INCHES				
PART	NO.	FUNCTION	thickness	×	width	×	length
A	2	supports	1		4		37
B	2	braces	1		3		24
C	1	rail	1		5		40
D	2	end panels	¾		18		22
E	2	rails	¾		2		37½
F	2	rails	¾		1¼		37½
G	18	dowels	⅜ diam.				15
H	1	bottom	½		16		37½
J	2	Masonite supports	¼		10		20

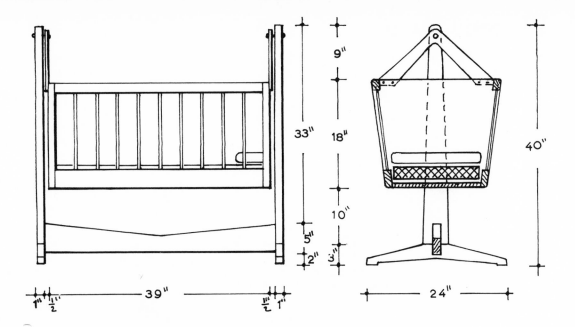

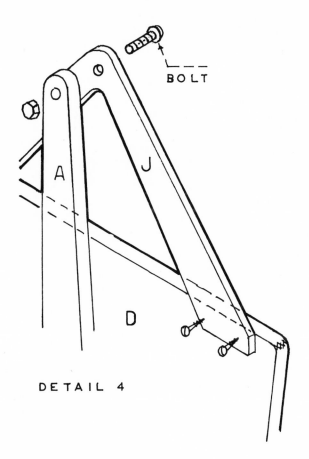

BOLT

DETAIL 4

Instructions for Assembly

1. Join supports (A) to braces (B) and attach cross-rail (C).
2. Insert dowels (G) in rails (E) and (F).
3. Fasten rails (E) and (F) to bottom (H) and to panels (D).
4. Attach supports (J) to panels (D) and supports (A).
5. Apply finish and add foam-rubber mattress.

Doll's Cradle

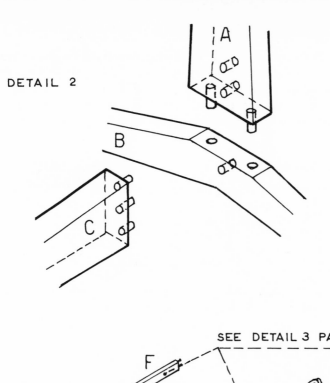

DETAIL 2

A

B

C

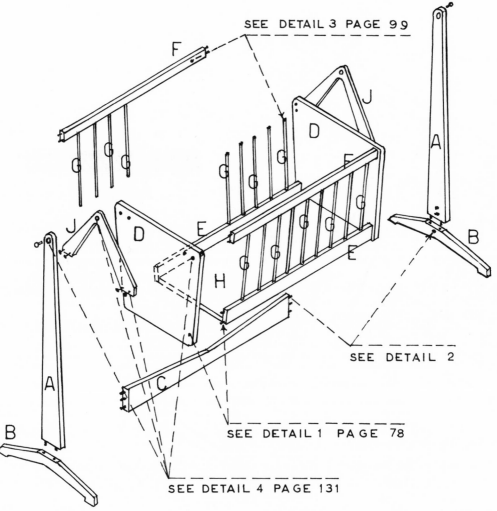

SEE DETAIL 3 PAGE 99

F

J

D

A

J

D

E

E

G G G

G G G

G

G G G G

G

H

G G G

E

B

A

C

SEE DETAIL 2

B

SEE DETAIL 1 PAGE 78

SEE DETAIL 4 PAGE 131

6.2 STANDARD CONSTRUCTION BLOCKS

The variety of imaginative structures that can be built with these blocks is almost endless. All you need is a power saw, a ruler and enough wood to make several dozen copies of each of the indicated pieces—more of the oblongs or "bricks," fewer of the circular pieces and columns. The big problem, of course, is to see that all pieces are stowed away when play is over! Avoid using soft wood, which has a tendency to split or splinter—try maple or birch for best results.

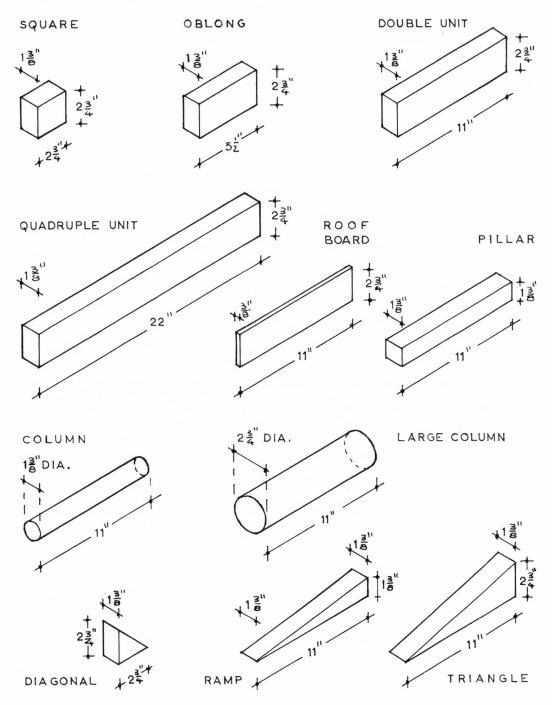

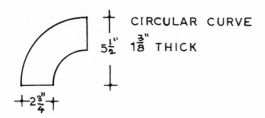

CIRCULAR CURVE

$5\frac{1}{2}''$ $1\frac{3}{8}''$ THICK

$2\frac{3}{4}''$

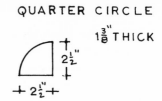

QUARTER CIRCLE

$1\frac{3}{8}''$ THICK

$2\frac{1}{2}''$

$2\frac{1}{2}''$

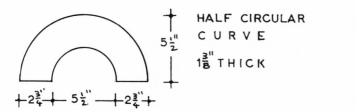

HALF CIRCULAR CURVE

$5\frac{1}{2}''$

$1\frac{3}{8}''$ THICK

$2\frac{3}{4}''$ $5\frac{1}{2}''$ $2\frac{3}{4}''$

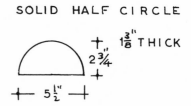

SOLID HALF CIRCLE

$1\frac{3}{8}''$ THICK

$2\frac{3}{4}''$

$5\frac{1}{2}''$

BUILDING

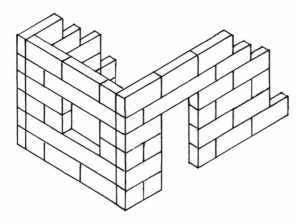

TUNNEL

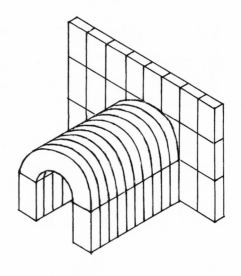

Standard Construction Blocks

6.3 DOLL HOUSE

This is the Number One project on any little girl's list. This design, though not as architecturally elaborate as some, will provide an endless amount of fun and fascination for juvenile homemakers. Scaled for use of plastic furniture readily available in dime stores.

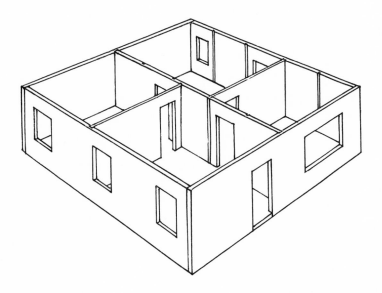

List of Materials

PART	NO.	FUNCTION	DIMENSION IN INCHES thickness × width × length		
A	1	front	½	8½	22
B	1	side	½	8½	21½
C	1	back	½	8½	22
D	1	side	½	8½	21½
E	1	bottom	½	21½	21½
F	1	partition	½	8	21½
G	2	partitions	¼	8	10½

Instructions for Assembly

1. Join bottom (E) to side (B) and side (D).
2. Fasten front (A) and back (C).
3. Install partitions (F) and (G).
4. Apply finish.

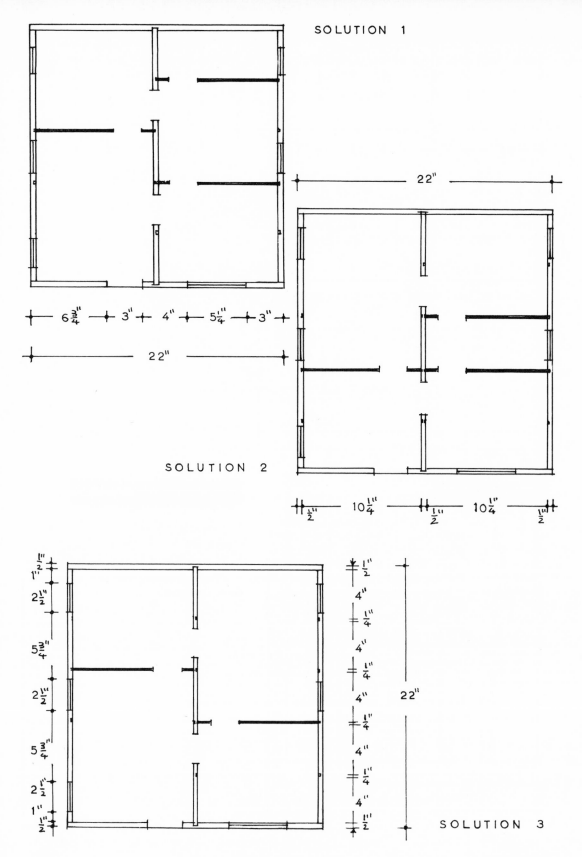

SOLUTION 1

SOLUTION 2

SOLUTION 3

Doll House

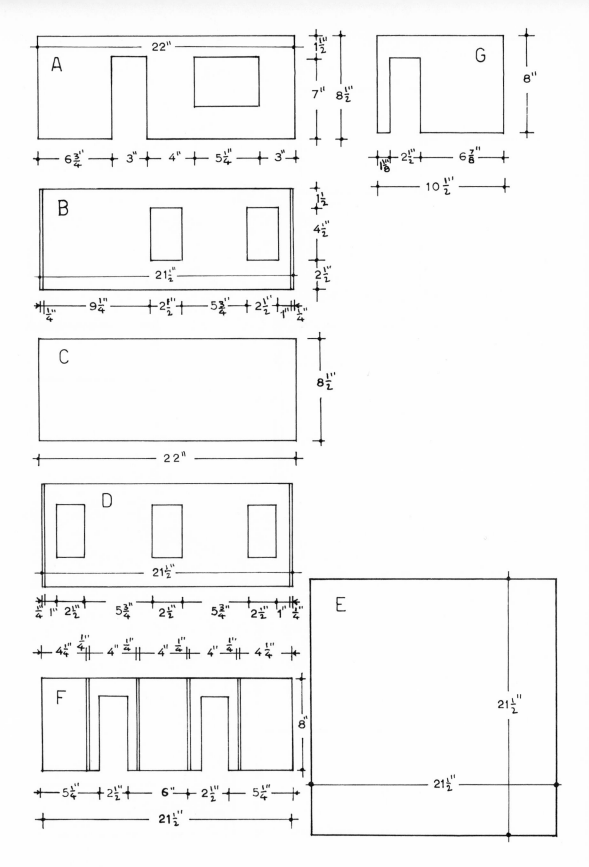

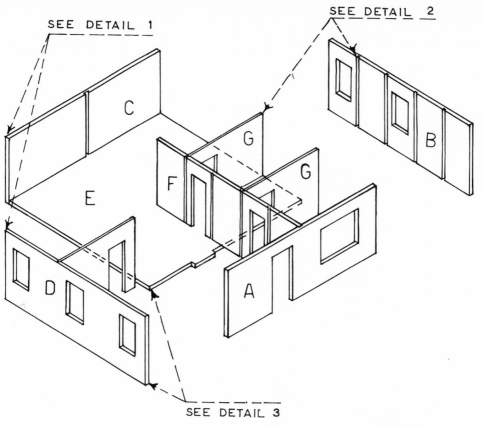

SEE DETAIL 1

SEE DETAIL 2

SEE DETAIL 3

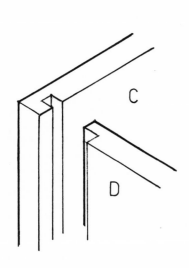

DETAIL 1

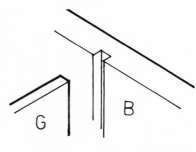

DETAIL 2

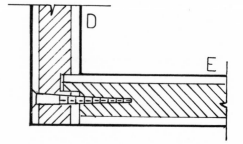

DETAIL 3

6.4 PAINTING EASEL

Encourages self-expression through drawing, while leaving the kitchen table uncluttered. The easel height can be adjusted to the child's growth. Spring clips at the top will hold a standard sheet of 18 × 24-in. drawing paper.

List of Materials

PART	NO.	FUNCTION	thickness	×	width	×	length
					DIMENSION IN INCHES		
A	4	supports	1		2		50
B	4	rails	1		2		23
C	1	panel	¾		26½		27
D	1	rail	2		3½		26½
E	1	Masonite panel	¼		23½		27
F	1	board	¾		3½		25½
G	1	strip	½		1		26½
H	2	strips	½		1		3¾

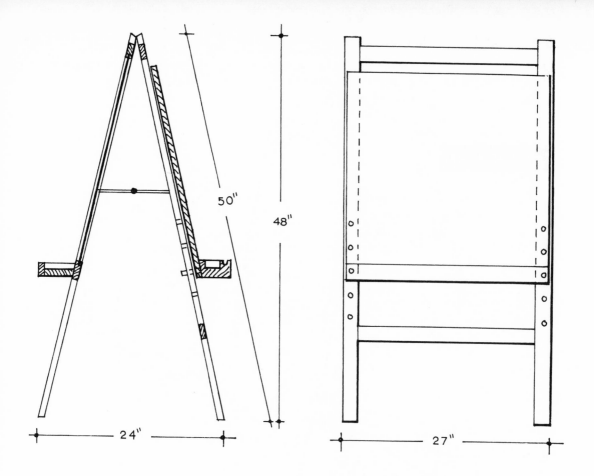

50"

48"

24"

27"

DETAIL 1

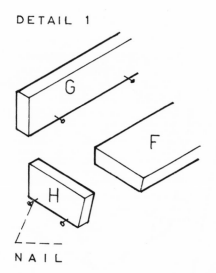

G

F

H

NAIL

1. Join supports (A) with rails (B) and install Masonite panel (E).
2. Attach rail (D) to panel (C).
3. Fasten strips (H) and (G) to board (F) and join to support (A).
4. Join supports (A) with hinge.
5. Apply finish and install adjustable panel (C).

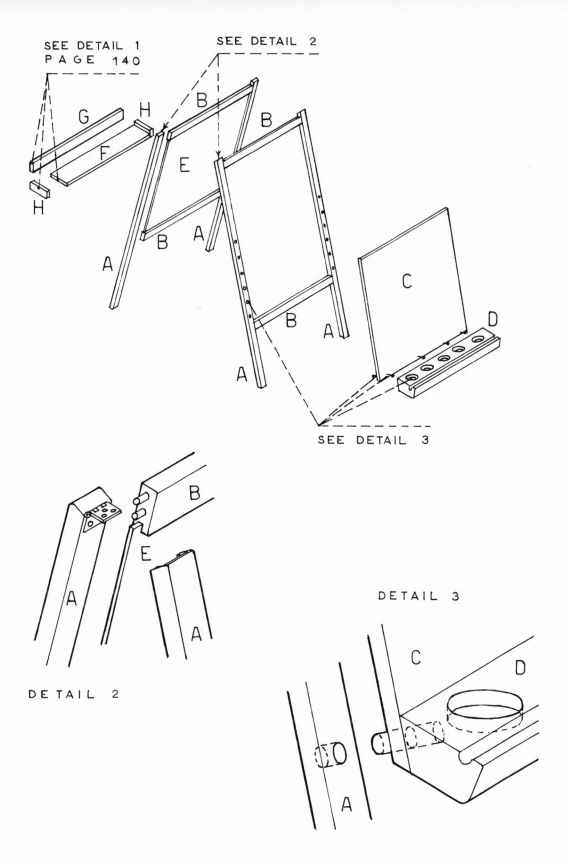

SEE DETAIL 1
PAGE 140

SEE DETAIL 2

SEE DETAIL 3

DETAIL 2

DETAIL 3

6.5 FOLDING PLAYHOUSE

This three-sided, folding, roofless structure may not look like a castle, a firehouse, or a general store, but that's because we left out the principal ingredient—the child's gift of imagination. If used outdoors (against the side of the house) it should be painted.

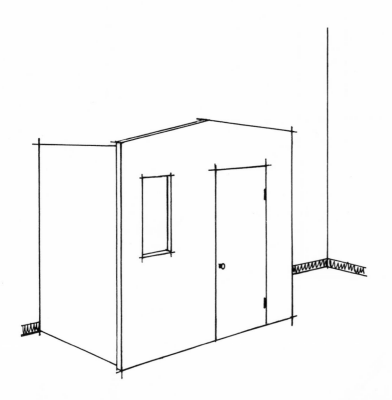

PART	NO.	FUNCTION	DIMENSION IN INCHES thickness × width × length		
A	1	front panel	¾	60	60
B	2	sides	¾	27	55
C	1	door	¾	18	46
D	1	strip	½	1¼	60

Instructions for Assembly

1. Join sides (B) to front (A).
2. Fasten strip (D) to front (A).
3. Install door.
4. Apply finish.

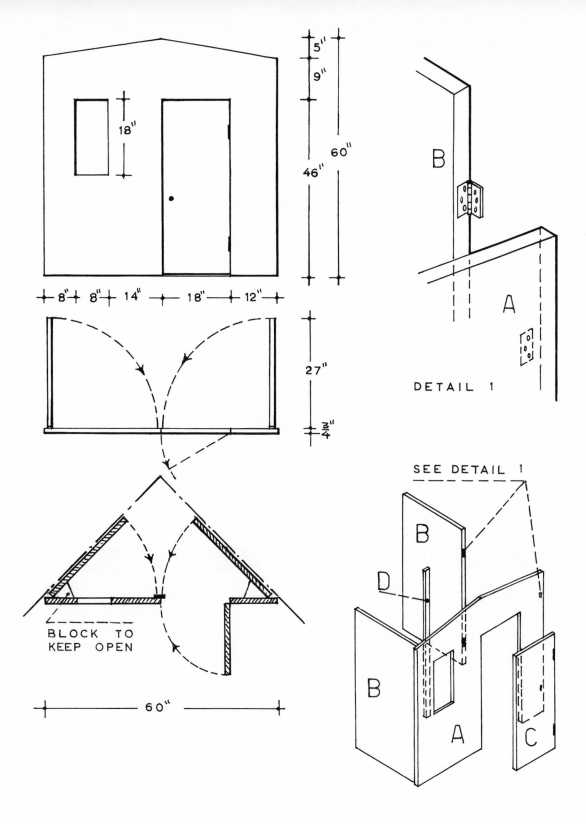

5"
9"
18"
46"
60"
8" 8" 14" 18" 12"
27"
3/4"
BLOCK TO
KEEP OPEN
60"

B
A
DETAIL 1

SEE DETAIL 1
B
D
B
A
C

6.6 HOCKEY TABLE

Hours of fun—and training in eye-hand coordination—are afforded by this simple table-top version of hockey. A children's game that can be shared by adults. A manufactured table, if at all available, would be pretty expensive, but this one takes only a little plywood and a few hours of your spare time.

List of Materials

PART	NO.	FUNCTION	DIMENSION IN INCHES thickness × width × length		
A	1	top	¾	23½	58½
B	2	strips	¾	1½	60
C	4	strips	¾	1½	10¾
D	4	corner blocks	¾	2	2
E	4	legs	¾	2	26
F	4	rails	¾	2	17
G	2	covers	¾	5	3½
H	4	folding metal supports			

Instructions for Assembly

1. Attach strips (B) and (C) to top (A) and install corner block (D).
2. Fasten covers (G) on strips (C).
3. Join legs (E) to rails (F).
4. Fasten legs (E) to top (A) and install metal supports (H).
5. Apply finish.

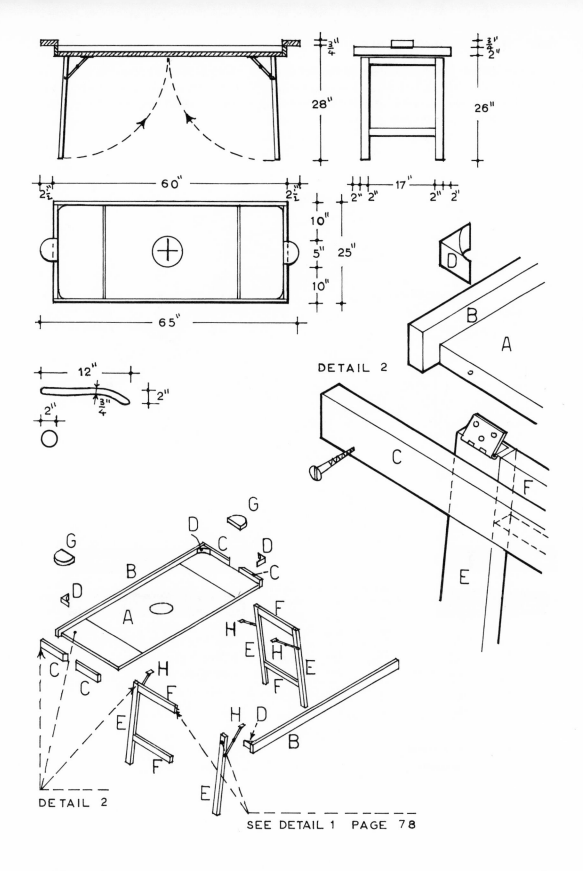

DETAIL 2

DETAIL 2

SEE DETAIL 1   PAGE 78

6.7 PING PONG TABLE

"Ping Pong" is actually a trademark or trade name for a special make of tennis table, but it has become so much of a household word that our use of it here can be excused. This is another family item which Dad and Mom will enjoy as much as the children. Construction is no problem—top of plywood, legs of solid wood, and a net-and-clamp set (from the local sports store), presto! You're ready for the first serve.

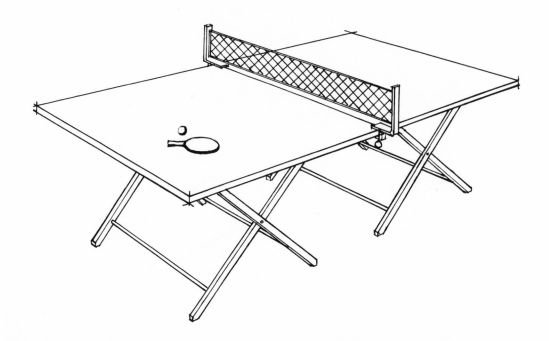

List of Materials

PART	NO.	FUNCTION	DIMENSION IN INCHES thickness × width × length		
A	2	tops	¾	48	48
B	4	rails	1	2	29
C	8	legs	1	1¼	43
D	4	stretchers	¾ diam.		32 (approx.)
E	2	metal clamps			
F	1	net (5 in. high)			

Instructions for Assembly

1. Join tops (A) with hinges at center.
2. Attach legs (C) with bolts at center.
3. Fasten rail (B) with stretchers (D) to legs (C).
4. Join legs (C) to top (A).
5. Install clamps (E) on top (A), and string net taut.
6. Apply finish.

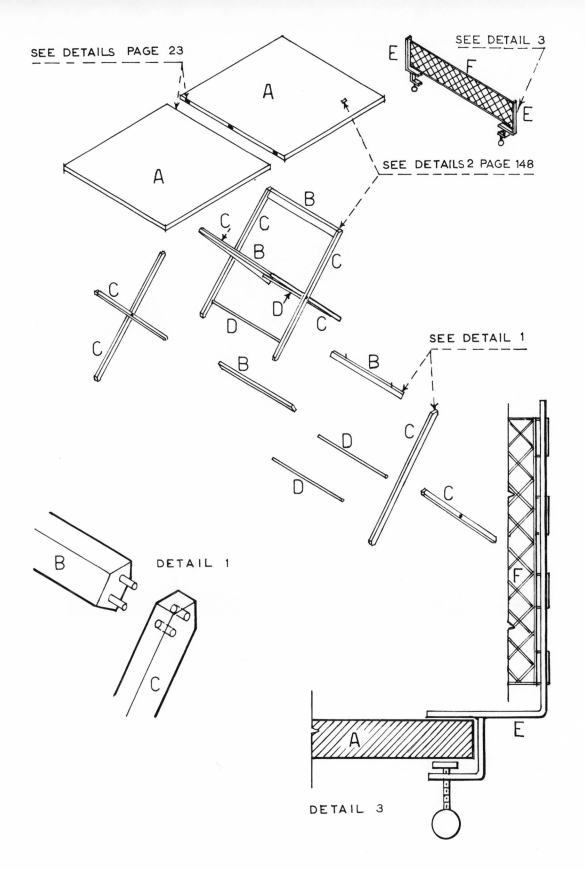

SEE DETAILS PAGE 23

A

A

A

SEE DETAIL 3

E

F

E

SEE DETAILS 2 PAGE 148

B

C

C

B

C

C

C

D

C

D

C

SEE DETAIL 1

B

B

C

D

C

D

C

B

DETAIL 1

C

F

C

E

A

DETAIL 3

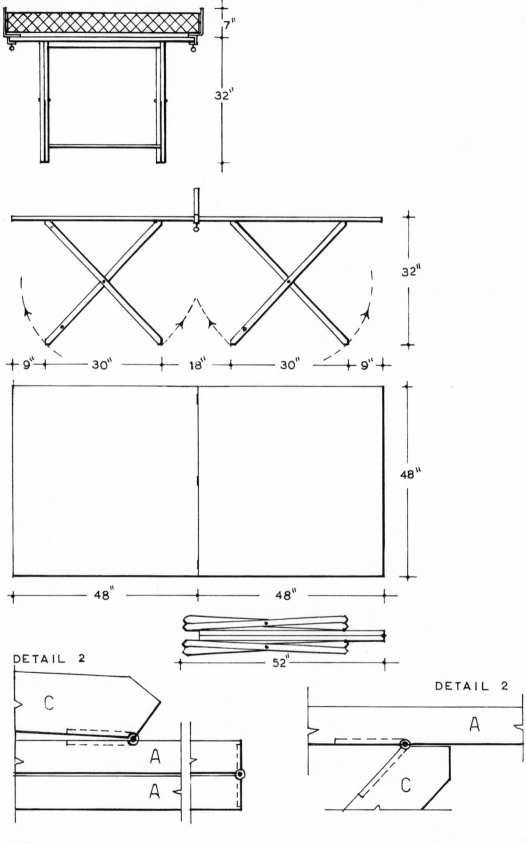

7"

32"

32"

9"   30"   18"   30"   9"

48"

48"   48"

52"

DETAIL 2

C

A

A

DETAIL 2

A

C

6.8 PUPPET THEATER

Punch and Judy, Kukla and Ollie, Lambchops and Charlie Horse will come to life in this child-size puppet theater, a training ground for the Burr Tillstroms and Shari Lewises of tomorrow. It just isn't fair to children *not* to build this plywood proscenium.

List of Materials

PART	NO.	FUNCTION	DIMENSION IN INCHES		
			thickness × width × length		
A	1	front panel	¾	28½	53
B	2	sides	¾	17	53
C	1	board	¾	2¾	28½

Instructions for Assembly

1. Join board (C) with front panel (A).
2. Install sides (B) by joining to front (A) with hinges.
3. Apply finish.

DETAIL 1

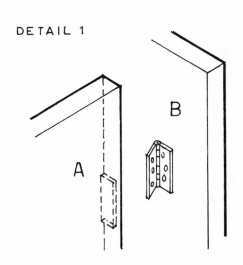

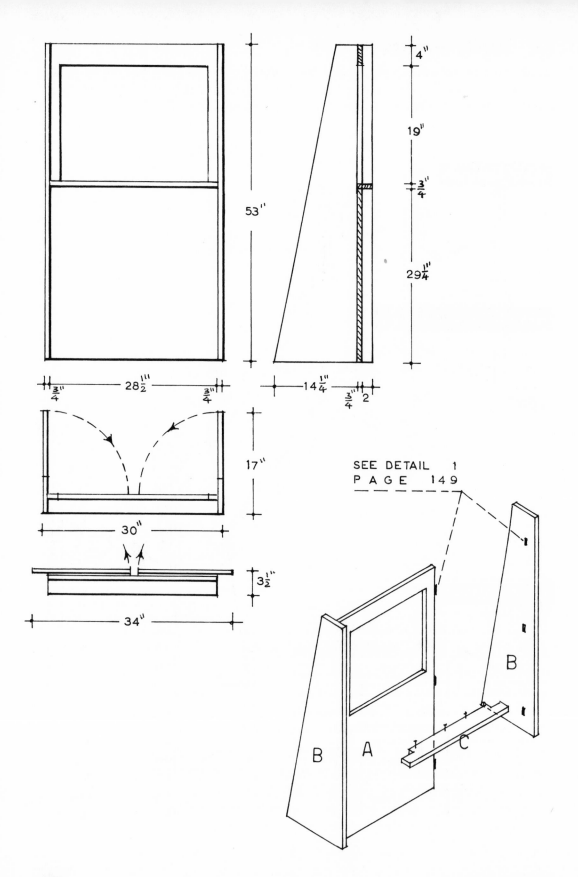

SEE DETAIL 1
P A G E 1 4 9

Puppet Theater

6.9 INDOOR-OUTDOOR SLIDE

Sturdy, exciting but safe for the toddler; the drop is only a foot and a half but the three-year-old will be thrilled. The slide is removable for easy carrying in and out of the house. Plenty of muscle-building activity indoors on rainy days with this low-cost equipment.

List of Materials

PART	NO.	FUNCTION	DIMENSION IN INCHES		
			thickness ×	width ×	length
A	4	supports	1½	1½	36
B	2	rails	1¼	1¾	17
C	4	dowels	1 diam.		20
D	1	rail	1¼	1¾	16
E	2	bottoms	1½	1½	36
F	2	sides	¾	3½	42
G	1	plank	¾	14½	42
H	2	side rails	1	1½	20
J	2	cross rails	1	1½	14¾
K	1	panel	¾	18½	20

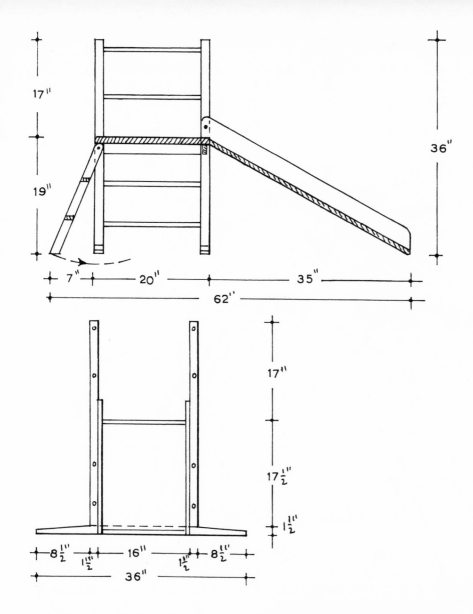

1. Join supports (A) to rails (B) and dowels (C).
2. Fasten supports (A) to rails (D) and (E) and attach panel (K).
3. Join sides (H) with rails (J) and attach sides (H) to (A) with screws.
4. Join sides (F) to sides (G).
5. Apply finish and install slide (F, G) by attaching to supports (A).

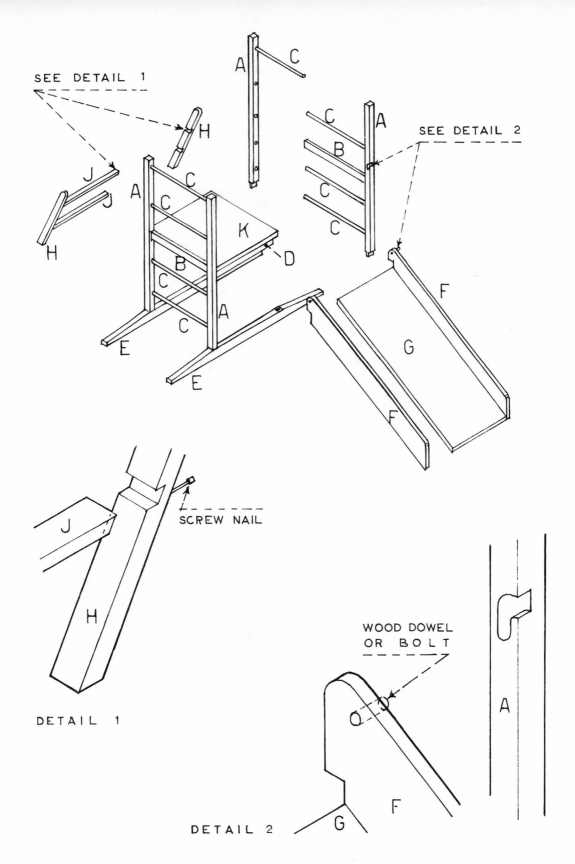

SEE DETAIL 1

A
C
H
A
C
C
K
A
B
C
C
D
E
E

SEE DETAIL 2

C
A
B
C
C

F
G
F

J
J
H

SCREW NAIL

J
H

DETAIL 1

WOOD DOWEL
OR BOLT

A
F
G

DETAIL 2

Indoor-outdoor Slide

6.10 LADDER BOX

For tots of a certain age, this can be the all-purpose fun machine par excellence. Stand it upright and it's an economy-size "monkey cage" like the one in the park; lay it on its side and it's a walk-through play pen or county jail; cover it temporarily with boards or sheets and it's a tent, an igloo, a fortress, an ogre's cave.

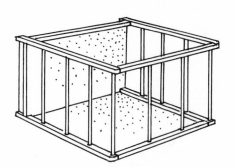

List of Materials

PART	NO.	FUNCTION	DIMENSION IN INCHES thickness × width × length		
A	4	legs	1½	1½	48
B	2	rails	1	1½	21
C	2	rails	1½	1½	45
C′	2	rails	1	1½	45
D	9	dowels	1 diam.		24
E	1	back panel	½	45	47
F	1	bottom	¾	23½	48
G	4	planks	½	5¼	48

Instructions for Assembly

1. Join legs (A) to rails (C) and (C′).
2. Fasten legs (A), rails (C, C′) and sides (B) with dowels (D).
3. Attach back (E) and bottom (F).
4. Apply finish.
5. Add planks (G) when box is used as a playhouse.

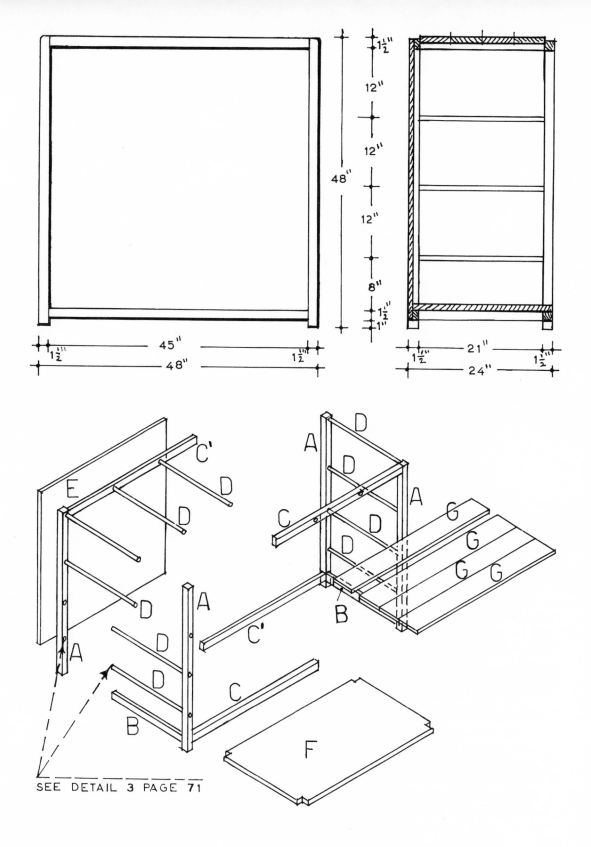

SECTION 7: OUTDOOR PLAY EQUIPMENT

7.1 OUTDOOR PLAYHOUSE and storage shed

As the above title indicates, this unit serves two distinct purposes—one at a time, of course. At first it is the exclusive property of the children—its use limited only by the imagination of the young people themselves. And when the summer days of childhood give way to the homework-ridden nights of the teen-ager, it can have a second life as a boy's workshop, storage shed for bikes and lawn mower, croquet equipment, ice skates, and the like.

List of Materials

PART	NO.	FUNCTION	thickness	×	width	×	length
A	4	planks	1		11⅝		76½
B	3	rails	2		2		46½
C	7	supports	1½		1½		62
D	2	supports	1½		1½		71
E	1	support	1½		1½		66
F	2	rails	1		2½		54
G	1	rail	1		2½		26
H	1	step	1		2½		26
J	2	rails	1		2½		23¼
K	2	rails	1		2½		24
L	4	cleats	¾		¾		62
M	3	boards	¾		8		54
O	2	rails	¾		3		23
P	1	Masonite panel	¼		45		84
Q	1	Masonite panel	¼		21		84
R	22	boards	¾		6¼		46½
S	20	boards	¾		6¼		76½

DIMENSION IN INCHES

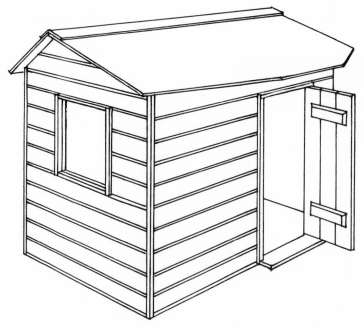

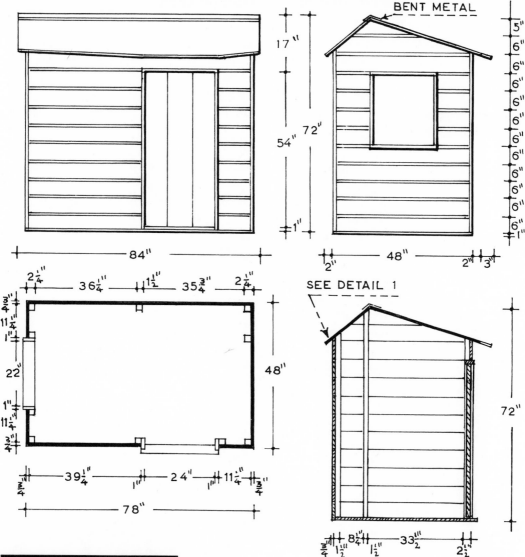

Instructions for Assembly

1. Connect floor (A) with rails (B).
2. Erect walls, joining boards (S) with supports (E) and fasten to floor.
3. Attach boards (R) to supports (C, D, E) and floor; cut space for window and door.
4. Install roof (P, Q) and fasten metal to it for water protection.
5. Attach rails (F) and (G) and bottom (H); assemble door and join rails (O) with boards (M) and rails (F).
6. Attach rails (J) and (K) to window, using clear polyethylene plastic film in place of glass.
7. Apply finish.

Outdoor Playhouse and Storage Shed

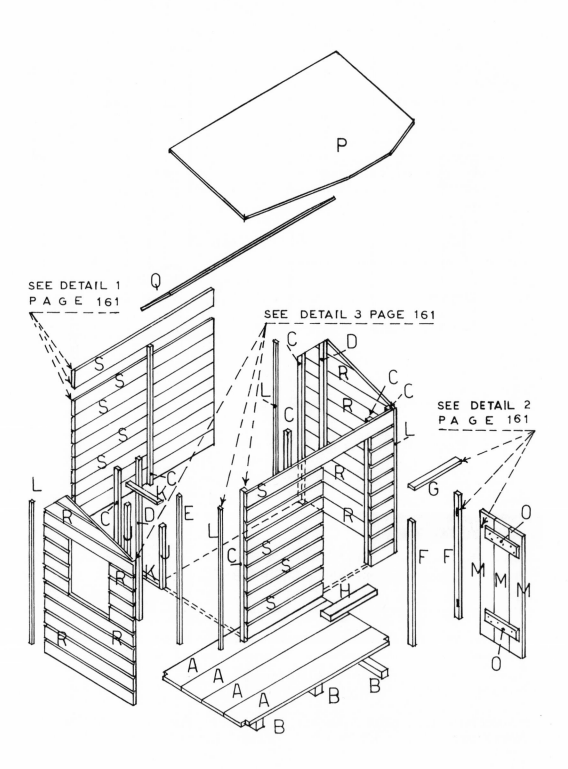

SEE DETAIL 1
P A G E 161

SEE DETAIL 3 PAGE 161

SEE DETAIL 2
P A G E 161

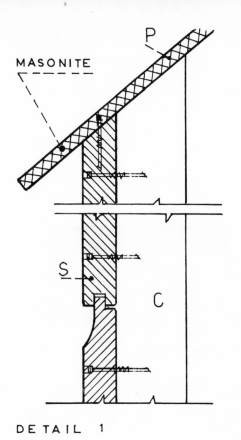

MASONITE

P

S

C

DETAIL 1

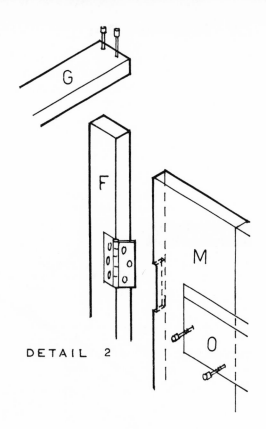

G

F

M

O

DETAIL 2

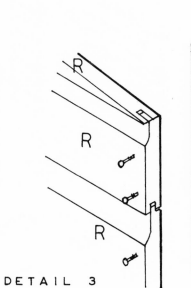

R

R

R

DETAIL 3

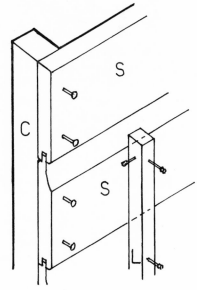

S

C

S

L

7.2 ROCKING BOAT

For dry-land sailors, junior grade, as well as owls and pussycats—as seaworthy as the *Enterprise* if the billows remain imaginary. The fearful trip done, our captain and crew become mountain climbers by the simple expedient of turning the craft over. Easy to make and easier to store.

List of Materials

PART	NO.	FUNCTION	DIMENSION IN INCHES thickness × width × length		
A	2	sides	¾	12	36
B	2	seats	¾	9	16½
C	2	partitions	¾	6	16½
D	1	bottom	¾	22	16½
E	2	dowels	1 diam.		18

Instructions for Assembly

1. Join seats (B) with bottom (D) and partitions (C).
2. Fasten sides (A) to seats (B), partitions (C), bottom (D) and dowels (E).
3. Apply finish.

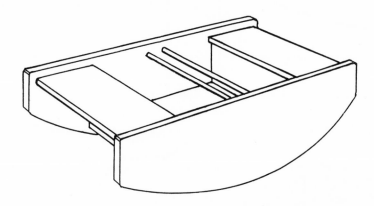

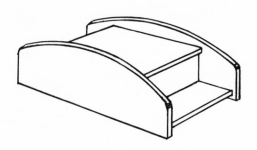

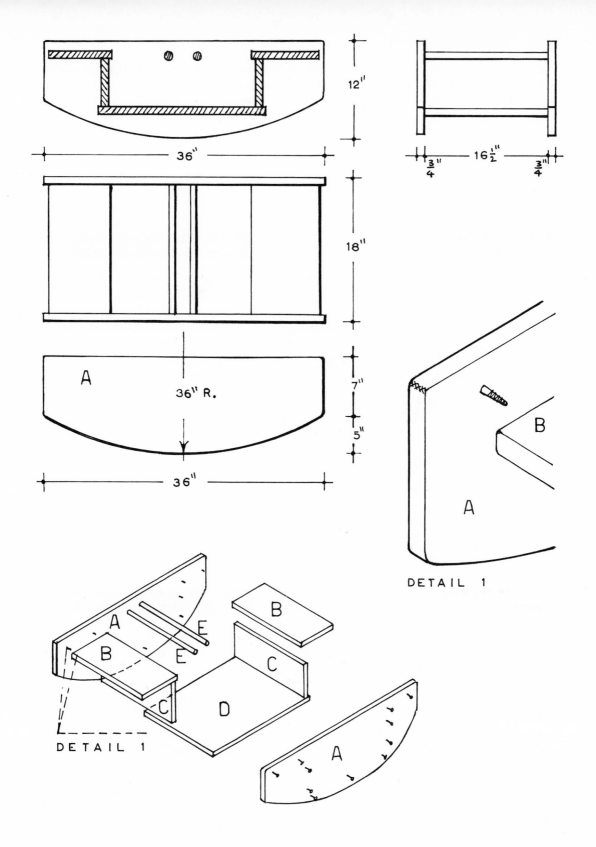

12"

36"

16$\frac{1}{2}$"

$\frac{3}{4}$"

$\frac{3}{4}$"

18"

A

36" R.

7"

5"

36"

B

A

DETAIL 1

A

E

B

E

B

C

C

D

A

DETAIL 1

7.3 TOBOGGAN

No toy this, but a full-scale, six-foot inflexible flyer for teen-agers hopeful of finishing second in the neighborhood Winter Olympics. Built of hardwood, such as beech or elm, that can be bent by steam and pressure to form the curved prow as indicated. You can make it seven or ten feet long if you wish!

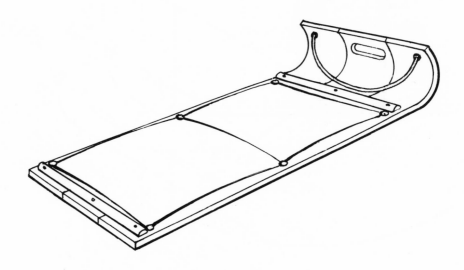

List of Materials

PART	NO.	FUNCTION	DIMENSION IN INCHES thickness × width × length		
A	3	boards	¾	5½	66 (or more)
B	2	half dowels	1½ diam.		15½
C	1	cushion	2	14	45 (or more)

Instructions for Assembly

1. Bend the three boards (A) using steam and pressure to indicated radius.
2. Join the three boards (A) together and attach dowels (B).
3. Apply finish.
4. Fasten cushion (C) to base with metal clips.

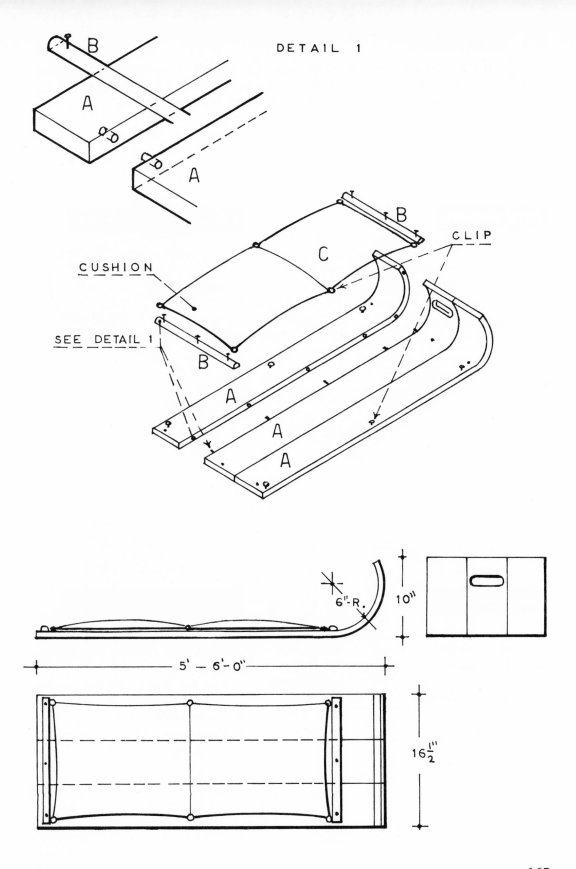

DETAIL 1

B

A

A

CUSHION

CLIP

C

B

B

SEE DETAIL 1

A

A

A

6" R.

10"

5' — 6'-0"

16½"

Toboggan

7.4 PARALLEL BARS

An inexpensive but serviceable version of the professional models found in high-school gyms, this exerciser will see a lot of muscle-building action before it is dismantled. Built in hardwood with tenon-and-mortise joints to withstand the vertical pressures.

List of Materials

PART	NO.	FUNCTION	DIMENSION IN INCHES thickness × width × length		
A	2	bars	2 diam.		78
B	4	supports	1½	2½	53
C	2	cross rails	1½	4	42
D	2	rails	1½	2½	62
E	4	cross rails	1¼	3½	19
F	4	corner blocks	1¼	7	7

(cut diagonally from two blocks)

Instructions for Assembly

1. Join supports (B) to rails (C) and (E).
2. Fasten rails (D) and bars (A) to supports (B) and attach corner blocks (F) to (B) and rails (D).
3. Apply finish.

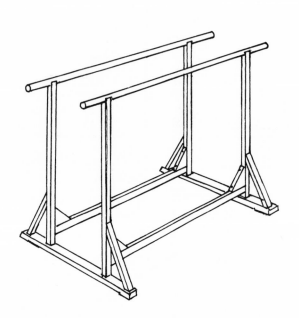

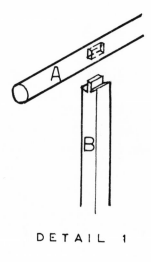

DETAIL 1

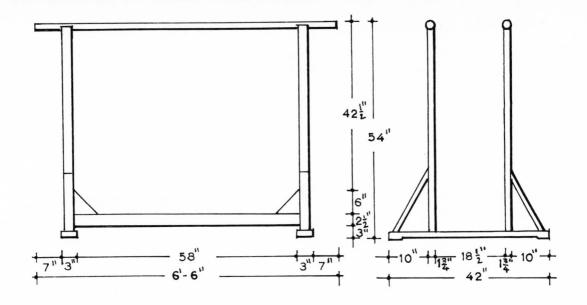

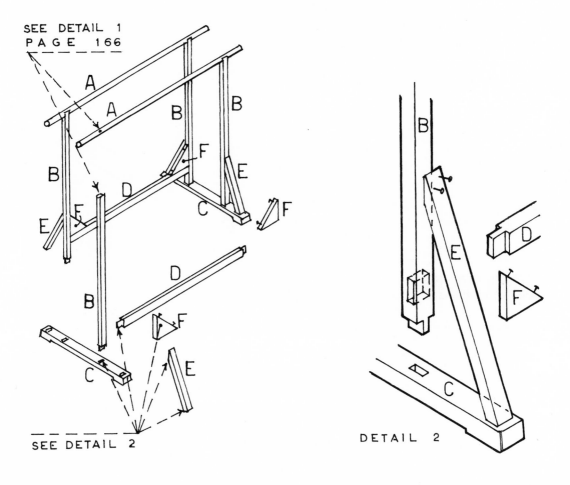

SEE DETAIL 1
PAGE 166

SEE DETAIL 2

DETAIL 2

Parallel Bars

7.5　HIGH BAR (for chinning)

Not intended for high jumps or pole vaults, since the crossbar is fixed in the holes. Its height is adjustable to accommodate a broad range of young athletes. The lumber for the uprights should be treated with creosote before the ends are placed in the ground. For increased safety and sturdiness, concrete footings are indicated.

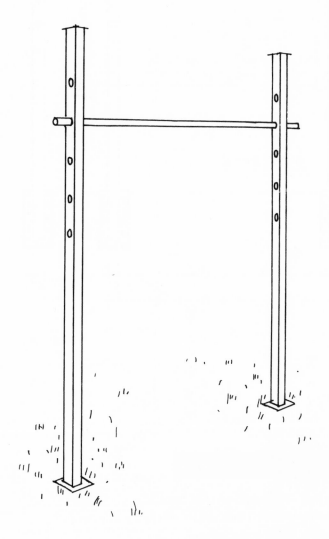

List of Materials

PART	NO.	FUNCTION	thickness	×	width	×	length
						DIMENSION IN INCHES	
A	2	supports	4		4		126
B	1	galvanized pipe 1–1 ¼ outside diameter					80
C	2	metal clips					

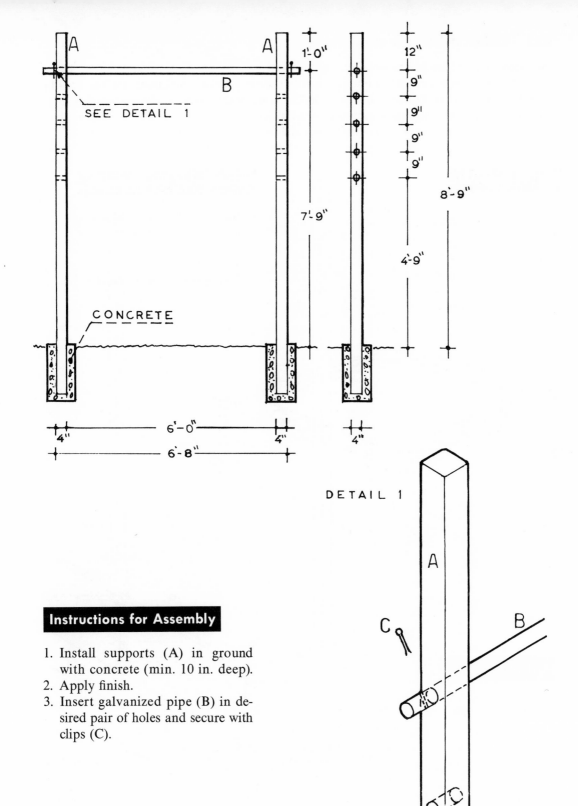

A
A
B
1'-0"
12"
9"
9"
9"
9"
8'-9"
SEE DETAIL 1
7'-9"
4'-9"
CONCRETE
4"
4"
4"
6'-0"
6'-8"

DETAIL 1

Instructions for Assembly

1. Install supports (A) in ground with concrete (min. 10 in. deep).
2. Apply finish.
3. Insert galvanized pipe (B) in desired pair of holes and secure with clips (C).

A

C

B

High Bar (for chinning)

7.6 TRAMPOLINE

Trampolines are becoming increasingly popular with the growth of outdoor pay-as-you-jump amusement centers. Here's one you can build in your own backyard, with no fee or time limit involved. Special care has been given to the safety features and strength of this unit, with resilient shock cables anchoring the nylon bed to the hardwood frame. Just the same, tell the kids to take it easy at first until they get the knack of it.

List of Materials

PART	NO.	FUNCTION	DIMENSION IN INCHES thickness × width × length		
A	8	rails	2	2	58
B	4	supports	2	2	18
C	4	corner blocks	1½	4	4
		(cut diagonally from two blocks)			
D	1	canvas sheet		48	48

Instructions for Assembly

1. Join rails (A) with supports (B).
2. Fasten corner blocks (C) to rails (A).
3. Apply finish.
4. Install canvas with nylon rope.

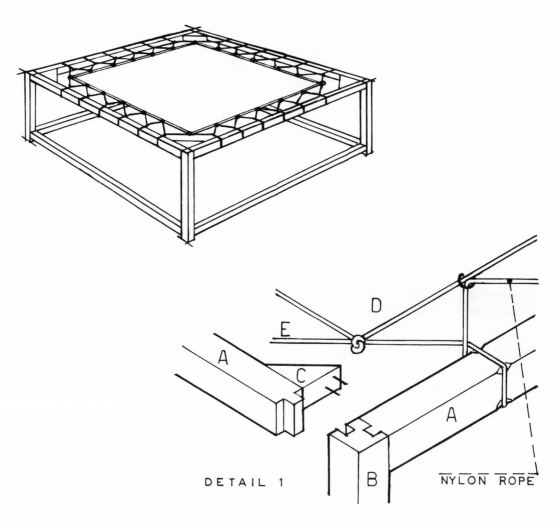

DETAIL 1

NYLON ROPE

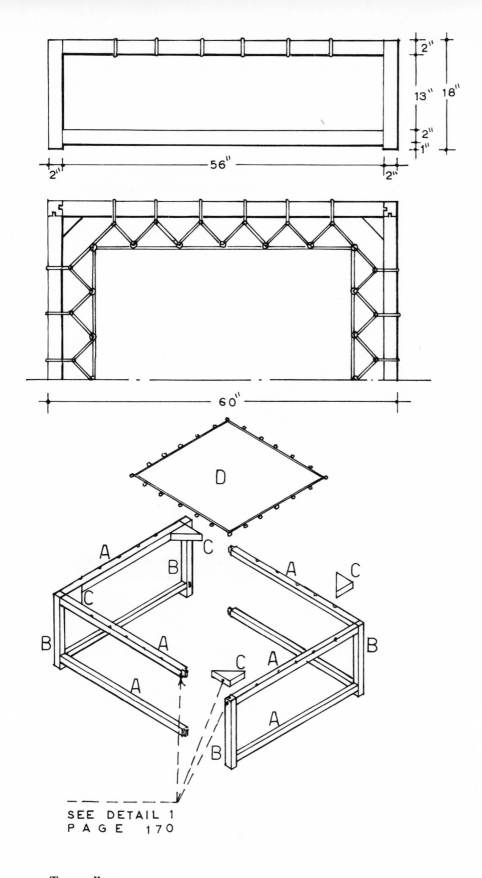

2"

13" 18"

2"
1"

56"

2" 2"

60"

D

A

B

C

C

A

C

B

A

A

B

A

C

A

A

C

B

A

SEE DETAIL 1
PAGE 170

Trampoline

7.7 SWING AND TRAPEZE with climbing bars

Here's a complete outdoor gymnasium for young folks, designed for safety as well as good fun and exercise. The four-by-four uprights will take all the bending stress a swinger can give them without the need for sway-bracing, which makes for a less cluttered appearance. Use nylon rope or approved swing chain rather than trusting to clothesline cord or other dubious substitute. As in other outdoor projects, treat ends of uprights before setting in concrete.

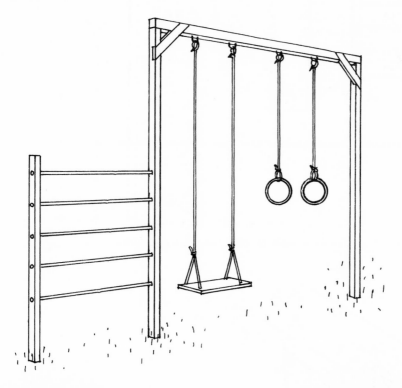

List of Materials

PART	NO.	FUNCTION	DIMENSION IN INCHES		
			thickness	× width ×	length
A	2	supports	4	4	168
B	1	support	4	4	115
C	1	cross support	4	4	120
D	2	cross rails	1½	3	27
E	4	lengths of nylon rope or chain			
F	1	seat	1	8	22
G	2	metal rings	8 diam.		
H	5	bars	2 diam.		56
J	6	bolts with headrings			

Instructions for Assembly

1. Join supports (A) to crossbar (C) and rails (D).
2. Insert supports (A) and (B) in ground with concrete after treating ends.
3. Fasten crossbars (H).
4. Install bolts (J) and attach seat (F) and rings (G) with nylon rope or chain (E).
5. Apply finish.

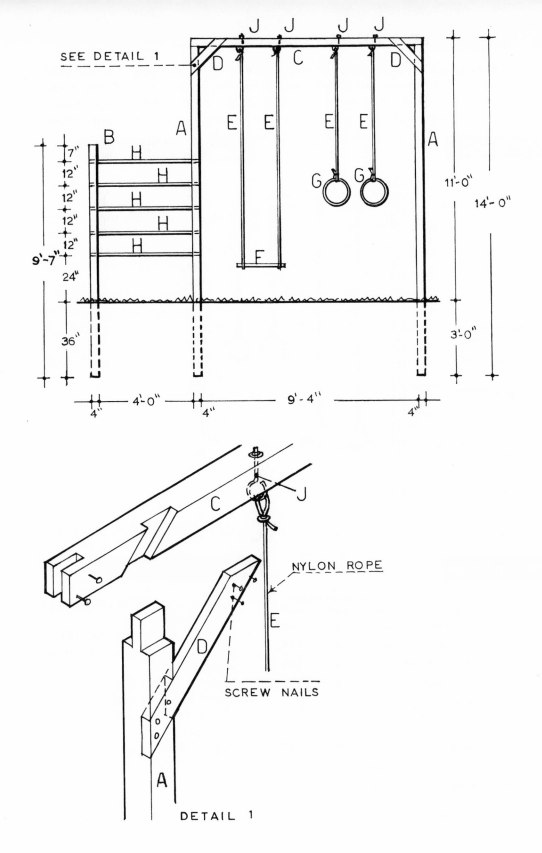

7.8 SWING, LADDER AND SEESAW

This well-liked preschool and kindergarten combination, useful up to about six or seven years, provides lots of fun and brightens up any backyard. As with all wooden exercise equipment, sandpaper all surfaces to guard against chance splinters and possible injury.

List of Materials

PART	NO.	FUNCTION	DIMENSION IN INCHES thickness × width × length		
A	4	supports	2	4	100
B	1	cross support	2	4	108
C	2	cross rails	1¼	3	48
D	2	blocks	1	8	8
E	2	supports	1¼	3	93
F	5	dowels	1 diam.		18
G	1	plank	1	8	96
H	1	block	1½	8	8
J	1	back	¾	8	14½
K	2	sides	¾	8	13
L	1	bottom	¾	12¼	14½
M	1	length of nylon rope or chain, 12 ft long			
O	4	metal rod	⅜ diam. × 21″ long		

Instructions for Assembly

1. Join supports (A) together and with cross rails (C) and blocks (D).
2. Install dowels (F) in supports (E).
3. Insert supports (A) and (E) in ground (using concrete) and attach cross support (B) blocks (D) and metal rod (O).
4. Join seat or bottom (L) with back and sides (J, K), and attach nylon rope or chain (M) to sides (K) and cross support (B).
5. Install plank (G) and attach block (H).
6. Apply finish.

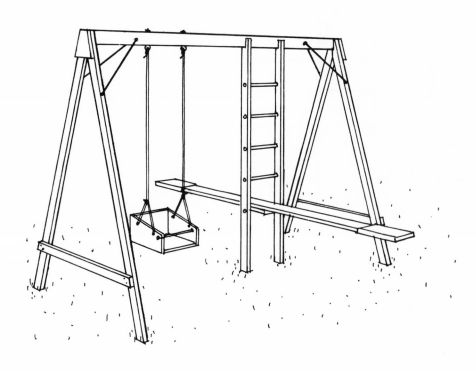

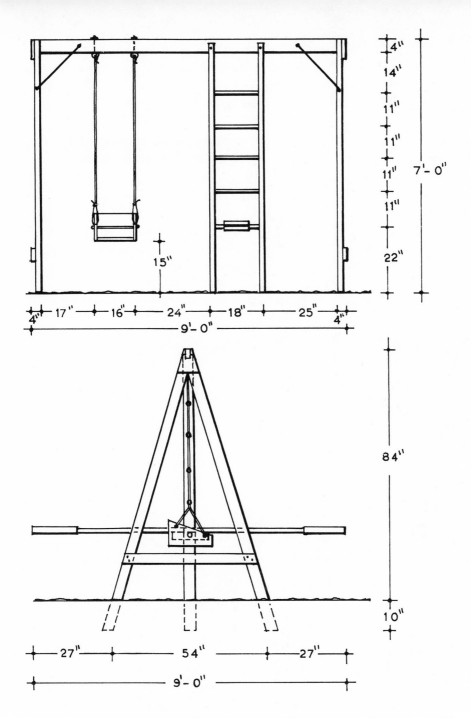

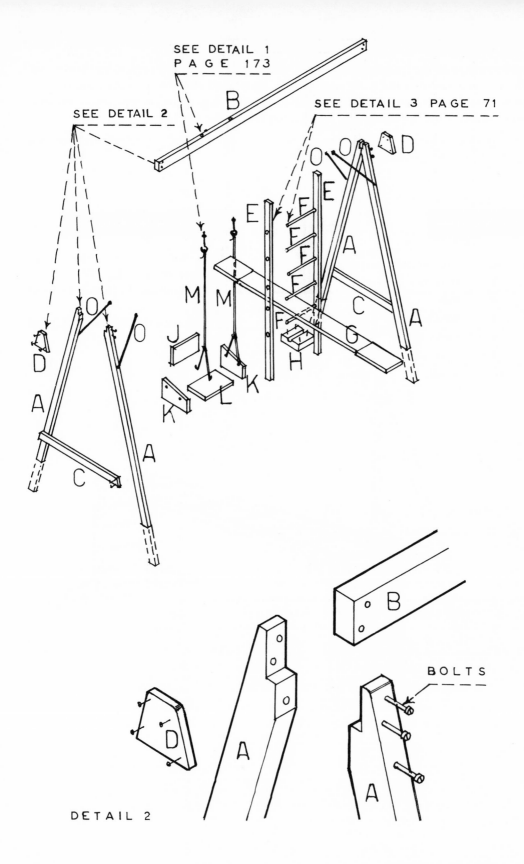

SEE DETAIL 1
PAGE 173

SEE DETAIL 2

SEE DETAIL 3 PAGE 71

BOLTS

DETAIL 2

7.9 THREE-WAY LADDER

Another version of the "monkey-cage" idea, this securely supported vertical and horizontal ladder is high enough in the horizontal span to allow small children to swing from rung to rung without danger, and to hang upside down with legs through the rungs—thereby building muscles and appetites. Use selected hardwoods for this one.

List of Materials

PART	NO.	FUNCTION	DIMENSION IN INCHES thickness × width × length		
A	2	cross rails	1½	3	96
B	4	rails	1½	3	49
C	2	bottoms	1½	5	48
D	4	corner blocks	1½	5	11
E	4	cross rails	1½	2	24
F	16	dowels	1 diam.		18

Instructions for Assembly

1. Join cross rails (A) with rails (B) and attach rails (E).
2. Install dowels (F) in rails (A) and (B).
3. Fasten rails (B) to bottom (C) and attach corner blocks (D).
4. Apply finish.

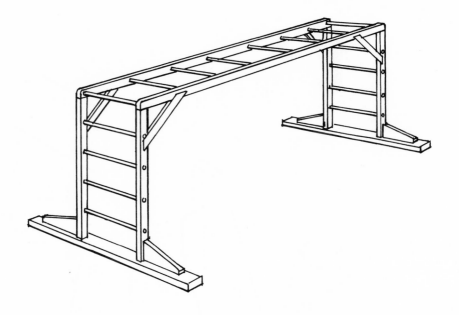

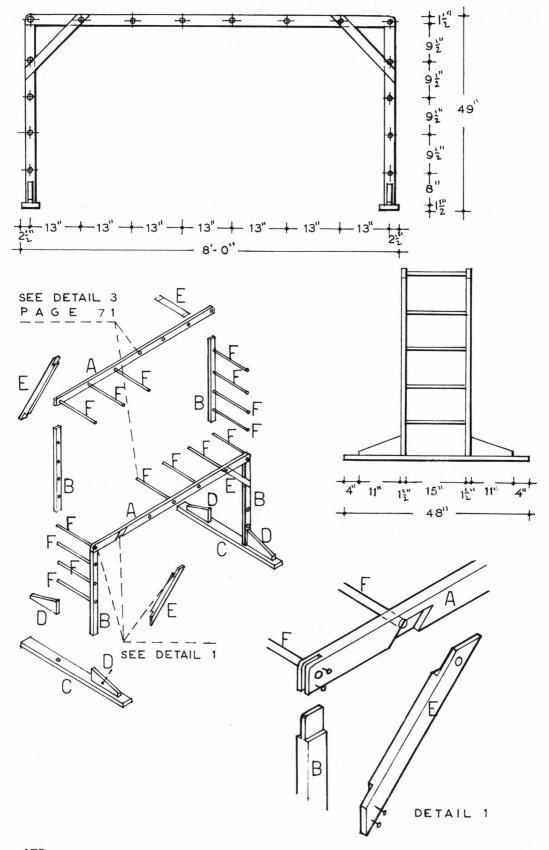

SEE DETAIL 3
P A G E 7 1

SEE DETAIL 1

DETAIL 1

49"

1½"
9½"
9½"
9½"
9½"
8"
1½"

2½" 13" 13" 13" 13" 13" 13" 13" 2½"

8'-0"

4" 11" 1½" 15" 1½" 11" 4"

48"

Three-way Ladder

7.10 SAND BOX

The endless fascination of the sand box for preschool children is well known to parents everywhere; no outdoor play area is complete without it. The awning is of plastic material and helps prevent sunburn in prolonged sandpile operations. It keeps the sand from getting wet on rainy days, too.

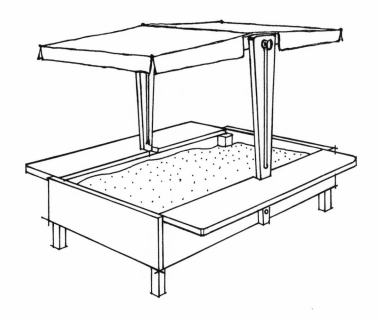

List of Materials

PART	NO.	FUNCTION	DIMENSION IN INCHES thickness × width × length		
			thickness	width	length
A	2	sides	¾	8¼	46½
B	1	front	¾	9	30
C	1	bottom	¾	28½	46½
D	4	legs	1½	1½	14
E	2	seats	¾	6¾	46½
F	2	supports	¾	5	40
G	2	sides	½	2½	48
H	2	rails	¾	2	28½
J	1	plastic sheet		36	72
K	4	corner blocks	1	2½	3½

Instructions for Assembly

1. Join sides (A) with bottom (C) and legs (D).
2. Attach front (B) to sides (A), bottom (C) and legs (D).
3. Fasten corner blocks (K) to seats (E) and sides (A).
4. Join rails (H) with sides (G).
5. Apply finish.
6. Install supports (F) and cover (J).

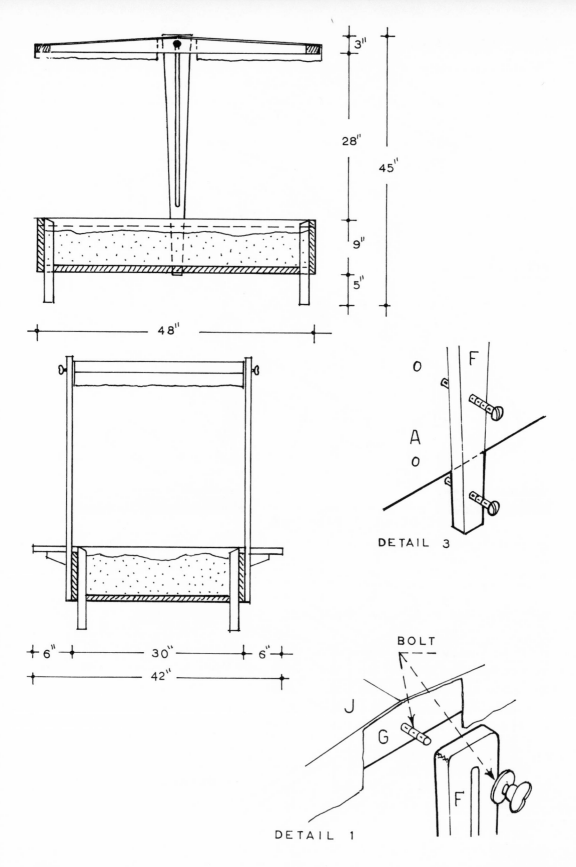

3"

28"

45"

9"

5"

48"

F

O

A

O

DETAIL 3

6"   30"   6"

42"

BOLT

J

G

F

DETAIL 1

Sand Box

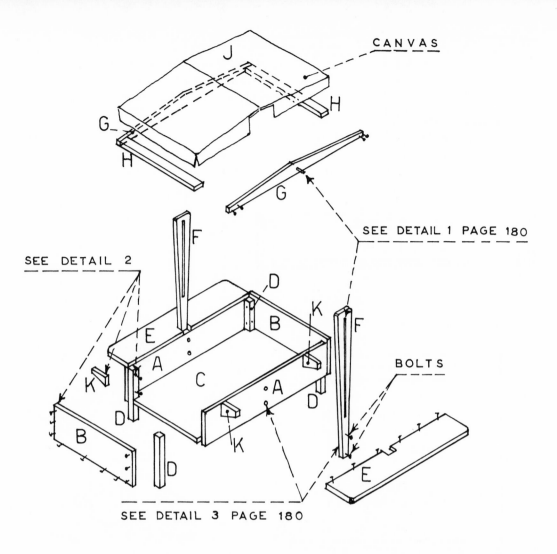

CANVAS

SEE DETAIL 1 PAGE 180

SEE DETAIL 2

BOLTS

SEE DETAIL 3 PAGE 180

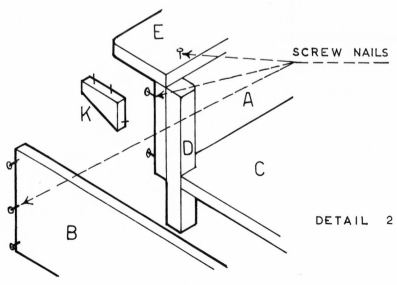

SCREW NAILS

DETAIL 2

Sand Box

7.11 OUTDOOR SLIDE

This is understandably more exciting than the slide of Project 6.9, having a drop of almost seven feet, which looks scary enough to six-year-olds. Not many slides as well built as this one are seen in backyards, and Dad will be justly proud of his handiwork.

List of Materials

PART	NO.	FUNCTION	thickness	×	width	×	length
					DIMENSION IN INCHES		
A	4	supports	1½		2½		90
B	1	panel	¾		18		21
C	2	bottoms	1¼		4		54
D	2	supports	1		2		33
E	1	rail	1		2		16
F	7	dowels	1 diam.				21
G	1	Masonite panel	¼		18		102
H	2	sides	1		5		120
J	6	cross rails	¾		1½		18
K	1	bottom	1¼		2½		36
L	2	supports	1¼		2½		18

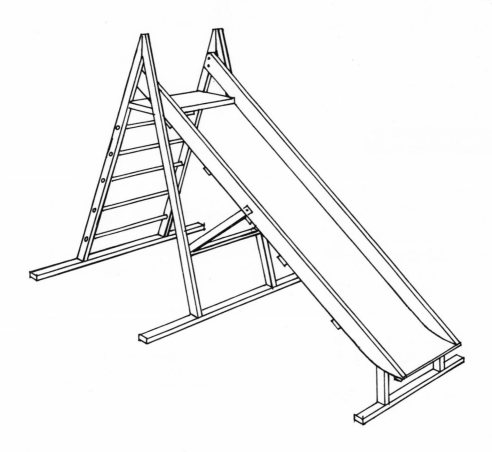

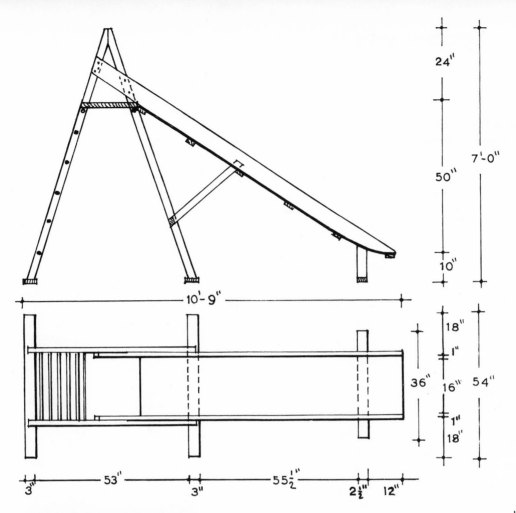

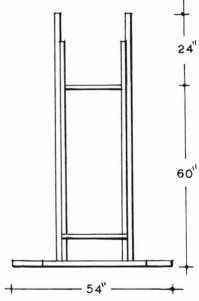

Instructions for Assembly

1. Join dowels (F) with supports (A).
2. Fasten supports (A) together with bolts and attach bottoms (C) and panel (B).
3. Attach panel (G) and support (J) to sides (H) and fasten latter to supports (A).
4. Fasten supports (L) to bottom (K) and sides (H).
5. Join supports (D) with cross rail (E) and supports (A) and sides (H).
6. Apply finish.

Outdoor Slide

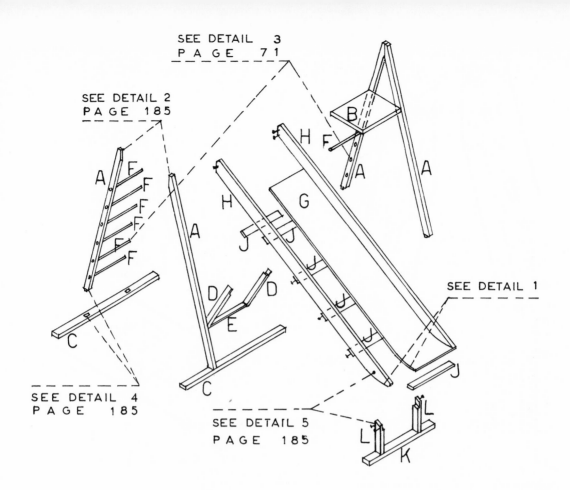

SEE DETAIL 3
PAGE 71

SEE DETAIL 2
PAGE 185

SEE DETAIL 1

SEE DETAIL 4
PAGE 185

SEE DETAIL 5
PAGE 185

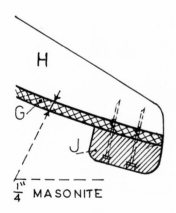

$\frac{1}{4}$" MASONITE

DETAIL 1

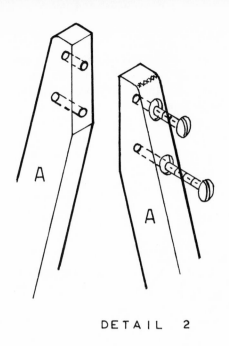

DETAIL 2

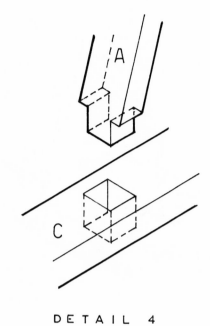

DETAIL 4

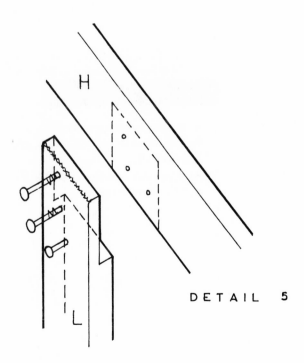

DETAIL 5

7.12 ROCK 'N ROWBOAT

Less nautical-looking than the boat of Project 7.2, this unit is bigger and affords more action per childpower. With a series of coordinated pushes and pulls the rock 'n rowboat can be made to "walk" along the ground, which is great fun even when the boat comes apart. The board is not fastened to either end, making storage a simple matter.

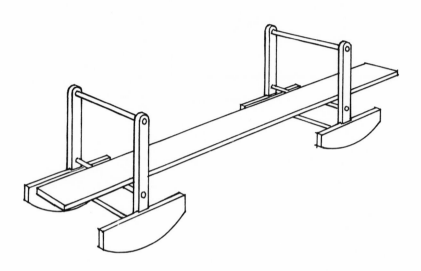

<table>
<tr><td colspan="3"></td><td colspan="3" align="center">DIMENSION IN INCHES</td></tr>
<tr><td>PART</td><td>NO.</td><td>FUNCTION</td><td>thickness</td><td>width</td><td>length</td></tr>
<tr><td>A</td><td>4</td><td>sides</td><td>1</td><td>7</td><td>21</td></tr>
<tr><td>B</td><td>4</td><td>rails</td><td>1</td><td>2</td><td>26</td></tr>
<tr><td>C</td><td>6</td><td>dowels</td><td>1 diam.</td><td></td><td>19</td></tr>
<tr><td>D</td><td>1</td><td>plank</td><td>1</td><td>9</td><td>90</td></tr>
</table>

List of Materials

PART	NO.	FUNCTION	thickness ×	width ×	length
A	4	sides	1	7	21
B	4	rails	1	2	26
C	6	dowels	1 diam.		19
D	1	plank	1	9	90

Instructions for Assembly

1. Join sides (A) with rails (B).
2. Fasten dowels (C) in sides (A) and rails (B).
3. Apply finish and insert plank (D) without fastening.

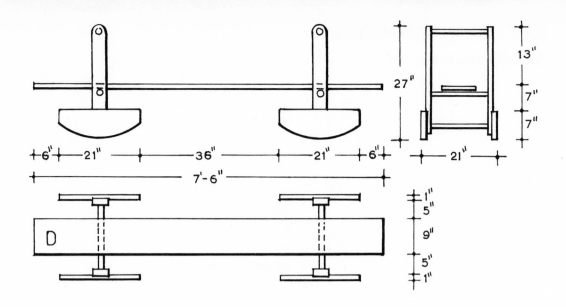

27"

13"
7"
7"

6" 21" 36" 21" 6"

7'-6"

21"

1"
5"
9"
5"
1"

D

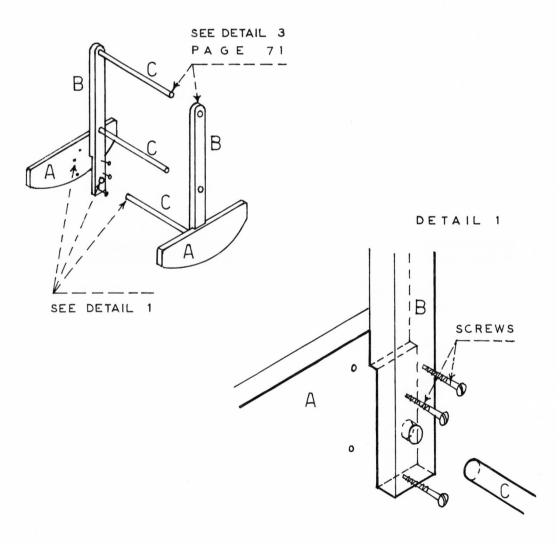

SEE DETAIL 3
PAGE 71

C

B

C

B

A

C

A

SEE DETAIL 1

DETAIL 1

B

SCREWS

A

C

7.13 COMBINATION SLIDE, SEESAW AND LADDER

Ingenious and versatile, for indoors and out, this final project will give you the greatest return for your efforts in terms of sheer fun. Here is one item that can be "handed down" as the family increases, and it's not likely to wear out with reasonable care. Easy to make, easy to carry, easy to store, it's the answer to the baby-sitter's problem of how to entertain Junior.

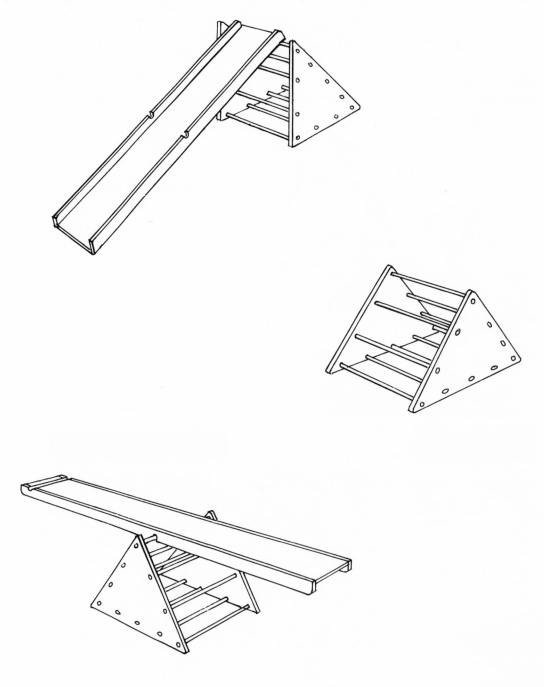

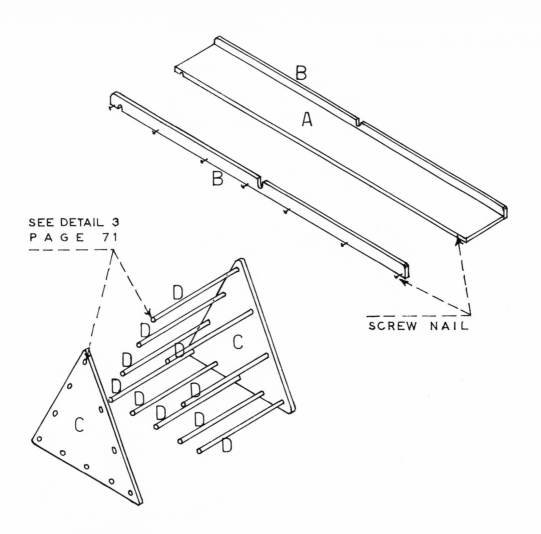

SEE DETAIL 3
PAGE 71

SCREW NAIL

List of Materials

PART	NO.	FUNCTION	DIMENSION IN INCHES thickness × width × length		
A	1	plank	¾	12	72
B	2	sides	1	2¾	72
C	1	panel	¾	27	27
		cut diagonally to form two triangles			
D	10	dowels	1 diam.		20

Instructions for Assembly

1. Fasten plank (A) to sides (B).
2. Join dowels (D) with sides (C).
3. Apply finish. *Note:* Make sure groove on back of slide is fitted over dowels when plank is used for either slide or seesaw.

Combination Slide, Seesaw and Ladder

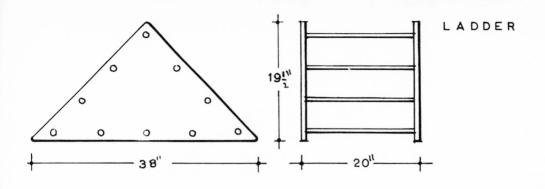

LADDER

$19\frac{1}{2}''$

$38''$

$20''$

PLANK

$2\frac{3}{4}''$

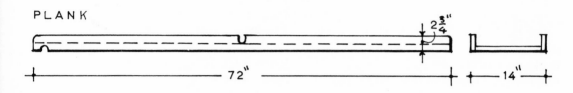

$72''$

$14''$

SLIDE

$27''$

$27''$

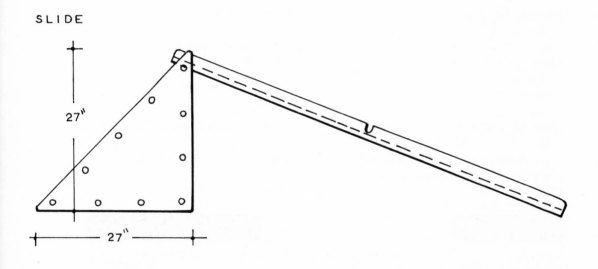

SAW HORSE

$72''$

$\frac{1}{2}''$

$19''$

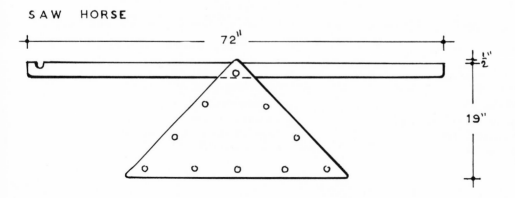

Combination Slide, Seesaw and Ladder

INDEX